I0018433

Build Your Own Linux-Powered Website

Full Setup & Management Guide

Written by, Lynne Kolestar

Table of Contents

Introduction

Overview of the Book

In this book, you'll learn how to set up, manage, and maintain a powerful Linux-based web server that can host both static websites (ideal for business connections) and dynamic websites (perfect for home use). Starting from the ground up, you'll be guided through every step: configuring your server for website hosting, securing it with HTTPS, setting up your own email server or using a remote email service, and integrating key features like payment gateways, FTP, SSH, and print servers to automate invoicing. Whether you're creating a personal blog or an e-commerce site, this book provides clear, easy-to-follow instructions for building a professional, fully functional web environment. By the end, you'll have a secure, scalable website running on your own Linux server, giving you complete control over its setup and ongoing management.

Prerequisites

This book is designed for beginners and intermediates with a basic understanding of Linux and web development. While you don't need to be an expert, familiarity with key concepts like file systems, terminal commands, and basic networking will be helpful. If you're new to these topics, don't worry— this guide will carefully walk you through each step, explaining essential concepts along the way. For those looking to deepen their Linux knowledge, my book series *The Linux Server Mastery Series* is available on Amazon. A willingness to learn and experiment is essential, as setting up a server requires hands-on experience. Whether you're just starting or already have some Linux experience, this guide will help you develop your skills and gain confidence in managing a live server environment.

Why Linux for Web Hosting

Linux is the preferred operating system for web hosting, and for good reason. It's open-source, free, stable, and highly customizable, making it ideal for building scalable and secure websites. Linux supports a wide range of server software, including Apache, Nginx, MySQL, PHP, and much more, giving you the flexibility to choose the tools that best suit your website's needs. Moreover, Linux is known for its efficiency, minimal resource consumption, and strong security model, making it a reliable choice for hosting both static and dynamic websites. Whether you're working with a static site or integrating databases, content management systems, or custom applications, Linux ensures your server is both powerful and secure.

Setting up the Environment

Before diving into the setup, there are a few essential tools and pieces of equipment you'll need. First, you'll require a Linux server, which can be either a dedicated machine or a virtual private server (VPS). You can repurpose an older PC or use a new one, as long as it meets the basic hardware requirements, which will vary depending on the size and type of your website. For this guide, we'll focus on a typical VPS setup, which is affordable and highly customizable. You'll also need an internet connection that supports either a static IP (typically for business) or a dynamic IP (usually for home use)—either connection type will work for your website server. On the software side, this book covers key tools like SSH for remote access, Apache or Nginx for web hosting, MySQL for database management, and programming languages such as PHP and HTML. We'll walk you through the installation and configuration of each tool, ensuring you have a fully functional environment for hosting both static and dynamic websites.

Choosing the Right Linux Distribution

Selecting the right Linux distribution (distro) is an important first step in setting up your web server. Linux comes in many flavors, but some distributions are better suited for web hosting than others. Ubuntu, Debian, and CentOS are the most popular choices for web servers due to their stability, active support communities, and large ecosystem of server software.

Ubuntu: Known for its user-friendly interface and extensive documentation, Ubuntu is a great choice for beginners and experienced users alike. It has frequent updates and is supported by most web hosting tools. The official website for Ubuntu is https://ubuntu.com.

Debian: Renowned for its stability, Debian is often the preferred choice for mission-critical web servers where reliability is paramount. The official website for Debian is https://www.debian.org.

CentOS: A derivative of Red Hat Enterprise Linux, CentOS is well-suited for high-performance and enterprise environments, offering a robust, long-term solution for hosting websites. The official website for CentOS is https://www.centos.org.

Each of these distros has its strengths, and in this chapter, we'll help you decide which one is best for your needs, guiding you through installation and setup.

Server Setup and Basic Configuration

After selecting and installing your preferred Linux distribution, booting up your system, and logging in, you're ready to begin configuring your server. The initial setup tasks include configuring the web server to support both HTTP and HTTPS for static and dynamic IP connections, setting up PHP with PDO, configuring MySQL and PDO, setting up an email server, configuring an FTP server, and enabling SSH access for secure remote management.

Chapter 1: Configuring Your Web Server Environment

Understanding Static and Dynamic IPs

In this chapter, we explore the concept of Static IPs and why you might choose to configure a static IP address for your Linux web server. Unlike Dynamic IP addresses (assigned by DHCP, which can change over time), a static IP is a fixed address that never changes, providing a consistent point of contact for other devices and services on the network. For a web server, having a static IP is essential because it ensures that your website remains accessible at the same address, regardless of changes to the network configuration. Additionally, a static IP is often necessary for setting up services like email servers, VPNs, or hosting multiple websites under different domain names on the same server. In this section, we'll discuss the advantages of using a static IP and explain why it's the preferred choice for most web hosting setups.

Before diving into these configurations, the first crucial step is to set yourself up as a sudo user. This grants you the necessary administrative privileges to execute root-level commands, ensuring you have full control over the system's configuration.

Step 1: Check if sudo is Installed

Log in to your server as the **root user**.

Run the following command to check if sudo is installed:

sudo -v

If sudo is installed, it will check for the sudo permissions.

If sudo is not installed, you will see an error message like:

command not found

Step 2: Install sudo (if not already installed)

If sudo is not installed, you can install it by following these steps, depending on your Linux distribution.

On Ubuntu/Debian-based systems:

Run the following command to install sudo:

sudo apt update

sudo apt install sudo

On CentOS/RHEL-based systems:

Run the following command to install sudo:

sudo yum install sudo

Step 3: Add a User to the sudo Group

Once sudo is installed, you need to give a user the ability to run commands with administrative privileges. By default, the users in the sudo group (on Debian-based systems) or wheel group (on Red Hat-based systems) are allowed to execute sudo commands.

Add a User to the sudo Group

Ubuntu/Debian-based systems: To add a user to the sudo group, run the following command, replacing username with the actual username:

sudo usermod -aG sudo username

Add a User to the wheel Group

CentOS/RHEL/Fedora-based systems: To add a user to the wheel group, run the following command, replacing username with the actual username:

sudo usermod -aG wheel username

Step 4: Verify the User's Sudo Permissions

After adding the user to the appropriate group, you can verify the changes by logging in with the user account and running a command with sudo:

sudo ls /root

If the user has been successfully added to the sudo or wheel group, the command will prompt you for the user's password and then show the contents of the /root directory.

Step 5: Configuring sudo (Optional)

By default, the sudo configuration is set to require the user's password when executing administrative commands. However, if you want to customize the sudoers file (such as disabling password prompts), you can do this by editing the /etc/sudoers file.

To edit the sudoers file safely, use the visudo command:

sudo visudo

This will open the sudoers file in the default editor and prevent syntax errors that could lock you out of sudo. You can make modifications here, such as granting passwordless sudo access for a specific user.

For example, to allow the user username to run sudo without entering a password, add the following line at the bottom:

username ALL=(ALL) NOPASSWD: ALL

Step 6: Apply Changes and Reboot (Optional)

After modifying user permissions or making changes to the sudoers file, it's a good practice to reboot the system to ensure everything is applied properly:

sudo reboot

Configuring Network Settings for a Static IP Connection

To configure a static IP on your Linux server, you need to modify the network interface configuration files specific to your Linux distribution. The process can vary slightly depending on whether you're using Ubuntu, Debian, or CentOS, but the core concepts remain the same.

Before You Start

If you don't know your assigned static IP, gateway, or nameservers, you can contact your ISP and ask for the following information:

What is my static IP?

What is my gateway?

What are my nameservers?

Alternatively, you can find these details directly from your Linux server using the following commands:

Finding Your Static IP Address - Run this command to view your network interfaces and IP addresses:

ip a

Look for the IP address associated with your network interface (e.g., eth0, ens33, wlan0).

It will look something like this:

inet 192.168.100.59/24

In this example, the static IP is 192.168.100.59.

Finding Your Nameservers - Run this command to check which nameservers are currently in use:

cat /etc/resolv.conf

The nameservers will be listed as nameserver followed by an IP address. They may look like this:

nameserver 8.8.8.8
nameserver 8.8.4.4

These are Google's public DNS servers, but your setup may vary based on your ISP.

Finding Your Default Gateway - To find your default gateway, which is needed to route traffic outside of your local network, use this command:

ip route

Look for the line starting with default via. It will look something like this:

default via 192.168.1.1 dev eth0

Here, 192.168.1.1 is the default gateway.

Once you have gathered your static IP, nameservers, and gateway, you can proceed with configuring the network interface.

In this section, we'll provide step-by-step instructions for each major distribution:

Ubuntu/Debian: The network settings are typically managed through the **Netplan** configuration (for newer versions) or the **/etc/network/interfaces** file (for older versions). We'll guide you through editing these files to assign a static IP address to your server.

CentOS/RHEL: For CentOS and Red Hat-based distributions, network configuration is typically managed through **NetworkManager** or the */etc/sysconfig/network-scripts/ifcfg- configuration files**. We'll cover the necessary changes to assign a static IP address. You will also learn how to configure the **subnet mask**, **gateway**, and **DNS servers**, which are necessary for proper network routing and domain name resolution. These settings allow your server to communicate with external networks, such as the internet, and resolve domain names to IP addresses.

Step-by-step setup:

Ubuntu/Debian (Netplan or /etc/network/interfaces)

Netplan Configuration (for newer versions of Ubuntu/Debian)

On Debian, **Netplan** is not installed by default, as Debian traditionally uses other network configuration tools like /etc/network/interfaces.

However, if you'd like to use **Netplan** on Debian (especially if you're more familiar with it from Ubuntu), you can install it manually.

Here's how:

sudo apt update

sudo apt install netplan.io

Create a Netplan Configuration File:

sudo nano /etc/netplan/01-netcfg.yaml

In this file, you can specify your network settings.

Here's an example configuration for a static IP (you may be using other interfaces such as enp0s3, eth1, or wlan0, depending on your system)**:**

```
network:
version: 2
renderer: networkd
ethernets:
eth0:
dhcp4: no
addresses:
- 192.168.1.100/24        # Your Static IP
gateway4: 192.168.1.1    # Your Default gateway
nameservers:
addresses:
- 8.8.8.8        # Google's Primary DNS (or use your own)
```

- 8.8.4.4   # Google's Secondary DNS (or use your own)

In newer versions of Ubuntu (18.04 and later), network settings are typically managed by **Netplan**.

Open the Netplan configuration file:

sudo nano /etc/netplan/00-installer-config.yaml

Modify the file to include your static IP settings. Here's an example configuration (you may be using other interfaces such as enp0s3, eth1, or wlan0, depending on your system):

network:
version: 2
renderer: networkd
ethernets:
eth0:
dhcp4: no
addresses:
- 192.168.1.100/24   # Your Static IP address
gateway4: 192.168.1.1   # Your Default gateway
nameservers:
addresses:
- 8.8.8.8   # Google's Primary DNS (or use your own)
- 8.8.4.4   # Google's Secondary DNS (or use your own)

Save and apply the configuration:

sudo netplan apply

Your server will now use the static IP address configured.

/etc/network/interfaces (for older versions of Ubuntu/Debian)

For older versions of Ubuntu/Debian, you need to modify the /etc/network/interfaces file.

Open the file for editing:

sudo nano /etc/network/interfaces

Add or modify the following lines to assign your static IP to an Ethernet interface (you may be using other interfaces such as enp0s3, eth1, or wlan0, depending on your system):

```
auto eth0
iface eth0 inet static
address 192.168.1.100     # Your Static IP
netmask 255.255.255.0     # Subnet mask
gateway 192.168.1.1       # Your Default gateway


# Use Google's DNS Servers (or use your own)
dns-nameservers 8.8.8.8  8.8.4.4
```

Restart the network service to apply the changes:

sudo systemctl restart networking

CentOS/RHEL (NetworkManager or /etc/sysconfig/network-scripts/)

NetworkManager (CentOS 7 and newer)

In CentOS 7 and newer versions, you can use nmcli to configure a static IP.

List your network interfaces:

nmcli connection show

Modify the connection to set a static IP (you may be using other interfaces such as enp0s3, eth1, or wlan0, depending on your system – if so, replace eth0 with your interface's name):

nmcli connection modify eth0 ipv4.addresses
192.168.1.100/24
nmcli connection modify eth0 ipv4.gateway 192.168.1.1
nmcli connection modify eth0 ipv4.dns "8.8.8.8 8.8.4.4"
nmcli connection modify eth0 ipv4.method manual
nmcli connection up eth0

/etc/sysconfig/network-scripts/ (CentOS 6 and older)

For older versions of CentOS, network settings are managed through the /etc/sysconfig/network-scripts/ directory.

Open the appropriate network configuration file for your interface (e.g., ifcfg-eth0):

sudo nano /etc/sysconfig/network-scripts/ifcfg-eth0

Add or modify the following settings:

```
TYPE="Ethernet"
BOOTPROTO="none"
IPADDR="192.168.1.100"     # Your Static IP
PREFIX="24"          # Subnet mask (24 means 255.255.255.0)
GATEWAY="192.168.1.1"      # Your Default gateway
DNS1="8.8.8.8"             # Your Primary DNS
DNS2="8.8.4.4"             # Your Secondary DNS
ONBOOT="yes"
```

Restart the network service:

sudo systemctl restart network

Subnet Mask, Gateway, and DNS Configuration

Subnet Mask: Defines the range of IP addresses available on your network. Common values are /24 (255.255.255.0).

Gateway: The IP address of the router that connects your local network to external networks (such as the internet).

DNS Servers: IP addresses of the servers responsible for resolving domain names (e.g., 8.8.8.8 is Google's DNS server).

These settings ensure that your server can properly communicate with external networks and resolve domain names.

Verifying Connectivity

After configuring the static IP, it's crucial to verify that your server is properly connected to the network and is accessible from other devices. In this section, we'll cover the steps to test and troubleshoot your static IP configuration:

Testing the IP address: Using commands like ifconfig (or ip in newer Linux versions) and ping, you'll verify that the static IP is correctly assigned to your network interface.

Verifying internet connectivity: We'll show you how to test external connectivity by pinging a well-known server (such as Google's DNS server at 8.8.8.8) to confirm that your server can reach the internet.

Troubleshooting common issues: If there are issues with the network configuration, we'll guide you through troubleshooting steps, such as checking the network interface status, reviewing configuration files, ensuring the network services are restarted, and using diagnostic tools like netstat and traceroute to identify potential problems.

Verify the IP Address Assignment

You can use either ifconfig (older versions of Linux) or ip a (newer versions) to check if your static IP address is assigned to the correct network interface.

Using ifconfig:

ifconfig

This will show details for all network interfaces on the system. Look for the network interface (e.g., eth0, ens33, wlan0) that you assigned the static IP to.

The output will look something like this if you are using the network interface eth0 (you could be using a different interface, such as enp0s3 or wlan0, depending on your system):

eth0: flags=4163<UP,BROADCAST,RUNNING,MULTICAST> mtu 1500

inet 192.168.100.59 netmask 255.255.255.0 broadcast 192.168.100.255

inet6 fe80::a00:27ff:fe1f:e0b9 prefixlen 64 scopeid 0x20<link>

ether 00:0c:29:f0:55:72 txqueuelen 1000 (Ethernet)

RX packets 5406 bytes 874642 (874.6 KB)

TX packets 6543 bytes 1235678 (1.2 MB)

In this example, 192.168.100.59 is the static IP assigned to the interface eth0.

Using ip a:

ip a

The output will display the assigned IP address for each network interface. You might be using a different interface, such as enp0s3 or wlan0, depending on your system.

Here's an example output:

2: eth0: <BROADCAST,MULTICAST> mtu 1500 qdisc fq_codel state UP group default qlen 1000

inet 192.168.100.59/24 brd 192.168.100.255 scope global dynamic eth0

valid_lft forever preferred_lft forever

inet6 fe80::a00:27ff:fe1f:e0b9/64 scope link

valid_lft forever preferred_lft forever

Step 2: Ping Your IP Address

Once you've confirmed that your static IP address is assigned, you can use the ping command to check if it's reachable.

Ping your own server - This will check if the network interface is responding on your server:

ping 192.168.100.59

You should see a response like:

PING 192.168.100.59 (192.168.100.59) 56(84) bytes of data.

64 bytes from 192.168.100.59: icmp_seq=1 ttl=64 time=0.053 ms

64 bytes from 192.168.100.59: icmp_seq=2 ttl=64 time=0.051 ms

If you receive a response, the static IP is working correctly.

Ping your gateway: Next, you can ping your default gateway to ensure that your server can communicate with devices outside your local network.

For example, if your gateway is 192.168.1.1, run:

ping 192.168.1.1

You should see something like:

PING 192.168.1.1 (192.168.1.1) 56(84) bytes of data.

64 bytes from 192.168.1.1: icmp_seq=1 ttl=64 time=1.23 ms

64 bytes from 192.168.1.1: icmp_seq=2 ttl=64 time=1.22 ms

Step 3: Ping an External Website (Test Internet Connectivity)

Finally, you can ping an external server, like Google's DNS server (8.8.8.8), to test internet connectivity:

ping 8.8.8.8

If you get a response, it means your server has access to the internet.

Example output:

PING 8.8.8.8 (8.8.8.8) 56(84) bytes of data.

64 bytes from 8.8.8.8: icmp_seq=1 ttl=54 time=10.1 ms

64 bytes from 8.8.8.8: icmp_seq=2 ttl=54 time=10.3 ms

Configuring Network Settings for a Dynamic IP

To configure a dynamic IP (DHCP) on your Linux server, you need to modify the network interface configuration files to tell the system to use DHCP to automatically receive an IP address from a DHCP server (typically your router or an external DHCP server).

Here's how you can configure it:

Ubuntu/Debian (Netplan or /etc/network/interfaces)

Netplan Configuration (for newer versions of Ubuntu/Debian)

On newer versions of Ubuntu/Debian, Netplan is the default tool to configure networking. If it's already installed, you can configure it to use DHCP.

Open your Netplan configuration file:

sudo nano /etc/netplan/00-installer-config.yaml

Modify it to look like this for DHCP:

```
network:
version: 2
renderer: networkd
ethernets:
 eth0:  # Replace with your network interface name
 dhcp4: true  # Enable DHCP for IPv4
```

Save and apply the configuration:

sudo netplan apply

Your system will now request an IP address from the DHCP server.

/etc/network/interfaces (for older versions of Ubuntu/Debian)

If you're using an older version of Ubuntu/Debian, you'll need to configure the /etc/network/interfaces file.

Open the file for editing:

sudo nano /etc/network/interfaces

Modify the configuration to request a dynamic IP:

auto eth0

iface eth0 inet dhcp # Use DHCP for dynamic IP assignment

Restart the networking service to apply the changes:

sudo systemctl restart networking

Your network interface should now obtain an IP address from the DHCP server.

CentOS/RHEL (NetworkManager or /etc/sysconfig/network-scripts/)

NetworkManager (CentOS 7 and newer)

On CentOS 7 and newer versions, you can use nmcli (NetworkManager CLI) to enable DHCP.

List your network interfaces:

nmcli connection show

Modify the connection to enable DHCP (replace eth0 with your actual interface name):

nmcli connection modify eth0 ipv4.method auto # Enable DHCP for IPv4

Bring the connection up:

nmcli connection up eth0

Now, the interface should obtain an IP address automatically from the DHCP server.

/etc/sysconfig/network-scripts/ (CentOS 6 and older)

For older versions of CentOS, network configuration is handled through /etc/sysconfig/network-scripts/.

Open the appropriate network configuration file for your interface (e.g., ifcfg-eth0):

sudo nano /etc/sysconfig/network-scripts/ifcfg-eth0

Ensure the following settings are present:

```
TYPE="Ethernet"
BOOTPROTO="dhcp"  # Enable DHCP for dynamic IP
ONBOOT="yes"     # Make sure the interface is activated on boot
```

Restart the network service:

sudo systemctl restart network

Your server should now be assigned an IP address automatically by the DHCP server.

Verifying the Dynamic IP Configuration

Once you've configured the network interface for DHCP, you can verify that the dynamic IP is correctly assigned using the following commands:

View IP Address

Run the following command to see the IP address assigned to your network interface:

ip a

You should see an IP address listed under the interface you configured (e.g., eth0, ens33, or wlan0).

Check Default Gateway

You can also verify that the default gateway is set:

ip route

Look for a line starting with default via, which indicates the default gateway.

Check DNS Configuration

To verify that DNS settings are being applied, check the contents of /etc/resolv.conf:

cat /etc/resolv.conf

This file should list the DNS servers assigned by the DHCP server.

Chapter 2: Web Hosting on Linux Servers (Static or Dynamic IP)

Understanding the Basics

In this chapter, we'll start by exploring the fundamentals of web hosting on a Linux server. A web server is a system that hosts websites, delivering content to users over the internet. Web hosting involves configuring a server to store the files that make up a website—such as HTML, PHP, CSS, JavaScript, images, and databases—and making them accessible to users online. Linux, an open-source operating system, has become the foundation for many web servers due to its flexibility, performance, and security. Understanding how web hosting works, and why Linux is the preferred choice for most server environments, is key to building your own web hosting setup.

Installation and Configuration of your Web Server (HTTP and HTTPS)

Here are step-by-step instructions for installing and configuring your web server on a Linux system with both HTTP (port 80) and HTTPS (port 443) support, using Apache as the web server and configuring SSL for secure HTTPS access.

Static IP Setup for Apache Web Server (HTTP and HTTPS)

When using a static IP, your server's IP address does not change over time. This simplifies the process, as your domain name (FQDN) can be directly mapped to the static IP.

Step 1: Install Apache Web Server

First, install Apache if it isn't already installed on your server.

sudo apt update

sudo apt install apache2

Step 2: Configure Apache to Listen on Ports 80 and 443 (HTTP and HTTPS)

Ensure Apache is configured to listen on both HTTP (80) and HTTPS (443) ports.

You can verify the configuration in the /etc/apache2/ports.conf file:

sudo nano /etc/apache2/ports.conf

Ensure the following lines are present:

Listen 80

Listen 443

Step 3: Create a Virtual Host for Your Domain

Next, you will configure a virtual host for your domain. Assuming your static IP is linked to your domain (e.g., mydomain.com), you will add a configuration for your domain.

Edit the default configuration file (or create a new one if necessary):

sudo nano /etc/apache2/sites-available/000-default.conf

Add or update the configuration:

```
<VirtualHost *:80>

    ServerAdmin webmaster@yourdomain.com

    ServerName yourdomain.com

    DocumentRoot /var/www/html

    ErrorLog ${APACHE_LOG_DIR}/error.log

    CustomLog ${APACHE_LOG_DIR}/access.log combined

</VirtualHost>
```

Step 4: Enable the Site and Restart Apache

Enable the virtual host and restart Apache to apply the changes.

sudo a2ensite 000-default.conf

sudo systemctl restart apache2

Your static IP should now be serving the website under the domain name for HTTP.

Step 5: Install Certbot for HTTPS (SSL) Configuration

Certbot is a tool that helps automatically configure SSL certificates from Let's Encrypt. When you run the installation and certificate generation process, it will prompt you for your Fully Qualified Domain Name (FQDN), which in this case is your domain (e.g., yourdomain.com).

Install Certbot

Use the following commands to install Certbot along with the Apache plugin:

sudo apt install certbot python3-certbot-apache -y

Step 6: Obtain an SSL Certificate

Once Certbot is installed, run the following command to

automatically obtain and configure an SSL certificate for your domain:

sudo certbot --apache

You'll be prompted to enter your email address for renewal notifications and asked to agree to the terms and conditions. Certbot will automatically detect your domain name and generate an SSL certificate for it.

After the process is complete, Certbot will configure Apache to use the new SSL certificate for HTTPS.

Step 7: Verify SSL Installation

You can now test HTTPS by navigating to your server's domain or IP address using https://:

For your static IP/domain: https://yourdomain.com

You should see the website served over HTTPS, with the browser showing a padlock icon next to the URL, indicating the connection is secure.

Step 8: Automate SSL Certificate Renewal

Let's Encrypt certificates are valid for 90 days, so it's important to set up automatic renewal. Certbot can handle this automatically by setting up a cron job.

To test the renewal process, run:

sudo certbot renew --dry-run

If the test is successful, Certbot will automatically renew the certificate before expiration, and Apache will be reloaded with the new certificate.

Step 9: (Optional) Force HTTPS Redirect

To force users to access your site over HTTPS, modify your Apache configuration file.

Open the configuration file:

sudo nano /etc/apache2/sites-available/000-default.conf

Add a redirect from HTTP to HTTPS by adding the following lines inside the <VirtualHost *:80> block:

<VirtualHost *:80>

    ServerAdmin webmaster@yourdomain.com

    ServerName yourdomain.com

    Redirect permanent / https://yourdomain.com/

```
</VirtualHost>
```

Save and exit (Ctrl + X, then Y, and Enter). Restart Apache to apply the changes:

sudo systemctl restart apache2

Now, visitors who try to access your site via HTTP will be automatically redirected to HTTPS.

Dynamic IP Setup Using No-IP and DDNS Client

If you're using a dynamic IP that changes periodically (which is common for home networks), you'll need to use a Dynamic DNS (DDNS) service to ensure your domain always points to your current IP. No-IP is a popular DDNS provider that can help with this.

Sign Up for a No-IP Account

Go to No-IP: Visit the **No-IP - https://www.noip.com/** website and create a hostname first then sign up for a **paid account**. A paid No-IP account allows you to use your **own registered domain name (e.g., yourdomain.com)** with their Dynamic DNS (DDNS) service.

Create a Hostname

Create a Hostname: After logging into your No-IP account, create a hostname. This hostname will point to your dynamic IP address.

For a free No-IP account: You will create a hostname like yourdomain.no-ip.org, which will automatically point to your dynamic IP.

For a Paid No-IP Account with a Custom Domain:

You can configure your custom domain (e.g., yourdomain.com) to point to your No-IP DDNS hostname yourdomain.no-ip.org, which will automatically update to your dynamic IP. This setup connects your registered domain (i.e. yourdomain.com) to your server via No-IP's DDNS service (e.g., yourdomain.no-ip.org), allowing you to use your custom domain for both your web server and email server.

Point Your Registered Domain to No-IP

After setting up a paid No-IP account, log in to your domain registrar and configure your domain to point to your No-IP DDNS hostname. This will link your registered domain to your Linux server using the No-IP service for dynamic IP updates.

Log in to Your Domain Registrar: Go to your domain registrar (e.g., GoDaddy, Namecheap, Google).

Create an A Record or CNAME Record: In the DNS management settings, create an **A record** or **CNAME record** for your domain (e.g., yourdomain.com) that points to the No-IP hostname you created (e.g., yourdomain.no-ip.org). This will direct traffic to your dynamic IP.

Install the No-IP Dynamic DNS Client

Download and Install the No-IP Client: Install the No-IP Dynamic DNS (DDNS) client on your Linux server to keep your DNS records updated with your dynamic IP address.

Open the terminal and run the following commands:

cd /usr/local/src

sudo wget https://github.com/no-ip/linux/releases/download/v2.1.9/noip-duc-linux.tar.gz

sudo tar xf noip-duc-linux.tar.gz

cd noip-2.1.9-1/

sudo make

sudo make install

Configure the No-IP Client

Configure the Client - After installation, run the configuration tool to set up the No-IP client:

sudo /usr/local/bin/noip2 -C

You'll be prompted to enter your No-IP account **username** and **password**. You will also need to specify the **hostname** (e.g., yourdomain.no-ip.org) you created earlier.

Start the No-IP Client

Start the Client - To begin updating your DNS records with your dynamic IP, run the following command:

sudo systemctl start noip2

To ensure that the No-IP client starts automatically on boot:

sudo systemctl enable noip2

Verify No-IP is Updating Your DNS

Verify the Client - To check that the No-IP client is updating your DNS records correctly, run:

sudo /usr/local/bin/noip2 -S

This will display the current IP address No-IP has assigned to your domain.

Important Note Your Fully Qualified Domain Name (FQDN)

FQDN: The hostname you created with No-IP (e.g., yourdomain.no-ip.org) will now serve as your Fully Qualified Domain Name (FQDN). You can use this FQDN to access your server, even with a dynamic IP address.

Install and Configure the Apache Web Server

Step 1: Update Your System

Before you install any software, it's a good idea to update your package lists to ensure that you have the latest versions of software packages.

sudo apt update && sudo apt upgrade -y

Step 2: Install Apache Web Server

Apache is one of the most widely used web servers on Linux.

To install Apache, run the following command:

sudo apt install apache2 -y

Once the installation is complete, Apache will start

automatically.

You can verify that Apache is running by checking its status:

sudo systemctl status apache2

You should see output indicating that the Apache service is active (running).

Step 3: Enable Apache to Start on Boot

To ensure that Apache starts automatically when the server boots up, run:

sudo systemctl enable apache2

Step 4: Adjust Firewall Settings

If you're using UFW (Uncomplicated Firewall), you need to allow HTTP (port 80) and HTTPS (port 443) traffic.

sudo ufw allow 'Apache Full'

This command allows both HTTP and HTTPS traffic through the firewall.

To verify that the firewall has been updated correctly:

```
sudo ufw status
```

Step 5: Check Apache Web Server

Once Apache is installed, you can test if it's working by navigating to your server's IP address in a web browser. Open a browser and enter:

```
http://your_server_ip
```

You should see the Apache2 default welcome page, confirming that the web server is up and running.

Step 6: Install SSL for HTTPS (Let's Encrypt SSL) for your dynamic IP setup

To secure your website with HTTPS, you'll need an SSL certificate. One popular way to get a free SSL certificate is by using Let's Encrypt.

Install Certbot

Certbot is a tool that helps automatically configure SSL certificates from Let's Encrypt. During the installation and certificate generation process, it will prompt you for your

Fully Qualified Domain Name (FQDN). The hostname you created with No-IP (e.g., yourdomain.no-ip.org) will now serve as your FQDN.

Install Certbot - Run the following commands to install Certbot and the Apache plugin:

sudo apt update

sudo apt install certbot python3-certbot-apache -y

Obtain SSL Certificate

Once Certbot is installed, you can automatically obtain and configure an SSL certificate for your domain.

Generate the SSL Certificate - Run the following command to request and install an SSL certificate for your domain:

sudo certbot --apache

During the process, you will be prompted to:

Enter your **email address** for renewal notifications.

Agree to **Let's Encrypt's terms and conditions**.

Certbot will automatically detect your domain and generate an SSL certificate for it.

Afterward, Certbot will configure Apache to serve the site over **HTTPS** using the newly obtained certificate.

Verify SSL Installation

Test HTTPS: To verify that HTTPS is working, navigate to your server's domain name using **https://**:

For the free no-ip account:

https://yourdomain.no-ip.org

For the paid Custom no-ip account:

https://yourdomain.com

You should now see the website served securely over HTTPS, indicated by the padlock icon next to the URL in your browser.

Automate SSL Certificate Renewal

Let's Encrypt certificates are valid for 90 days, so it's crucial to set up automatic renewal.

Test the Renewal Process - Certbot automatically sets up a cron job to handle renewals, but you can test the renewal process by running:

```
sudo certbot renew --dry-run
```

If the dry run is successful, Certbot will automatically renew your certificate before it expires, and Apache will reload with the updated certificate.

(Optional) Force HTTPS Redirect

To force users to access your site securely over HTTPS, you can configure Apache to redirect all HTTP requests to HTTPS.

Edit Apache Configuration - Open your Apache configuration file for the default site:

```
sudo nano /etc/apache2/sites-available/000-default.conf
```

Add the following lines inside the <VirtualHost *:80> block to redirect all HTTP requests to HTTPS:

```
<VirtualHost *:80>
    ServerName yourdomain.com
    Redirect permanent / https://yourdomain.com/
</VirtualHost>
```

Restart Apache - Save the file (press Ctrl + X, then Y, and Enter), and restart Apache to apply the changes:

```
sudo systemctl restart apache2
```

Now, users who attempt to access your site via HTTP will automatically be redirected to HTTPS.

Web Hosting Essentials (Static IP)

Next, we'll dive into the essentials of web hosting— understanding the role of domains and DNS (Domain Name System). A domain is the address users type into their browsers to access your website, while DNS translates domain names into IP addresses that servers use to communicate. In this section, we'll explain how to register a domain and configure it to point to your server.

Registering a Domain Name and Pointing it to your Linux Server for Static IP

Your IP address is assigned by your ISP. If your Linux server has a **static IP address**, it means the IP remains constant and doesn't change over time. Static IPs typically cost more and are often considered business-level connections by most ISPs. This makes domain configuration easier, as you can

directly register your domain and point it to your static IP without worrying about future updates or changes.

If you don't have a static IP address, then you have a **dynamic IP address**, which means your ISP periodically changes your IP. In this case, you'll need specific instructions to ensure your changing IP is properly pointed to your server. Refer to the section titled *Registering a Domain Name and Pointing it to Your Linux Server for Dynamic IPs* to continue.

Choose a Domain Name

Brainstorm: Think about what you want your domain name to represent. It should be short, memorable, and relevant to your website's purpose.

Consider Keywords: If applicable, try to include relevant keywords that relate to your business or personal brand.

Check Availability: Use a domain name checker tool (most domain registrars have one) to check if the domain name you want is available.

Select a Domain Registrar

A **domain registrar** is a company authorized to sell domain names.

Popular registrars include:

GoDaddy - https://www.godaddy.com/

Namecheap - https://www.namecheap.com/

Google Domains - https://domains.google/

Search for Your Domain Name

Go to the registrar's website.

Enter the domain name you want to register into the search bar.

The registrar will tell you if the domain is available or not. If it's taken, you may need to try a different name or a different

TLD (e.g., .com, .org, .net, .biz).

Select Your Domain Name and TLD

Choose a TLD: TLD stands for Top-Level Domain (like .com, .net, .org, .co, etc.).

Consider Alternatives: If your first choice isn't available, you can try using a different TLD or slightly modify the domain name to find an available option. You can also select a TLD that signifies your country, such as (.us for the USA, .ca for Canada, .uk for the UK, etc.).

Add Domain Privacy Protection (Optional)

Many registrars offer WHOIS protection or Domain Privacy Protection, which keeps your personal information (such as

your address and phone number) private in the public WHOIS database. This is a useful feature, as it helps protect you from being inundated with unsolicited business offers. This is optional but recommended to protect your privacy.

Create an Account with the Registrar

If you don't already have an account with the registrar, you'll need to create one.

This involves entering your personal details and setting up a payment method.

Add Your Domain to the Cart and Proceed to Checkout

Once you've selected your domain, you can proceed to checkout.

Most registrars offer domain registration for one year, with the option to extend the registration for multiple years.

Complete the Purchase

Provide your billing information and confirm the purchase. After completing the payment, you will have successfully registered your domain!

Verify Your Registration

After registration, the registrar will usually send you an email to verify your domain name registration. Be sure to confirm

it. You will also be listed as the domain owner in the WHOIS database.

Renew Your Domain

Domains typically need to be renewed annually. Keep track of your renewal dates to ensure you don't lose ownership of your domain.

After registration, you will need to login to your registrar to set up and configure your domain to point to your Linux Server's static IP address:

If you don't know your assigned static IP, you can always contact your ISP and ask for the following information:

What is my static IP?

What are my nameservers?

Alternatively, you can use the following commands on your Linux server to find out these details:

To find your static IP address:

ip a

Look for the IP address listed under your network interface (usually eth0, ens33, wlan0, or wlp2s0). It will look something like this: 192.168.100.59.

To find your nameservers:

cat /etc/resolv.conf

Your nameservers will be listed here and may look like this:

ns1.google.com

ns2.google.com

Or, they could be numeric, like:

8.8.8.8

8.8.8.9

This will display the nameservers your server is using.

Once you've determined your static IP address and nameservers, you can proceed to configure your domain by these steps:

Point your domain name to your Linux Server

Here's a general step-by-step guide for pointing a newly registered domain name to a static IP address on various domain registrars:

GoDaddy:

Log in to your GoDaddy account.

Go to "My Products" and click on **"Domains"**.

Find your domain and click on **"DNS"** or **"Manage DNS"** next to the domain name.

In the **DNS Management** section, find **"A (Host)"** record.

Click **"Edit"** next to the "A" record (if it exists) or add a new record.

Host: @ (This represents your root domain, e.g., example.com)

Points to: Enter Your Linux Server's **static IP address** here (e.g., 192.168.100.59).

TTL: Set to default or 1 hour.

Save Changes and wait for the DNS to propagate (this can take anywhere from a few minutes to 48 hours).

Namecheap

Log in to your Namecheap account.

Go to the **"Dashboard"** and click on **"Manage"** next to your domain.

Navigate to the **"Advanced DNS"** tab.

Under **"Host Records"**, locate the **A Record**.

Edit the **A Record** or add a new one:

Host: @ (this points to your root domain, e.g., example.com)

Value: Enter Your **static IP address** here (e.g., 192.168.100.59).

TTL: Set to "Automatic" or a preferred time.

Save Changes and wait for DNS propagation.

Google Domains

Sign in to your Google Domains account.

In the **"My Domains"** section, click **"Manage"** next to your domain.

Under the **"DNS"** tab, scroll to the **"Custom Records"** section.

Locate or create an **A Record**:

Name: @ (represents the root domain).

Type: A

TTL: Set to default (1 hour).

Data: Enter Your **static IP address** here (e.g., 192.168.100.59).

Save Changes and wait for propagation.

Note: Propagation can take from several hours to 24 hours.

Adding Your Nameservers

If your Linux server is not acting as a DNS service and you're simply hosting a website or other services on it, you don't need to run your own DNS server. Instead, you just need to point the domain to your server's static IP address by configuring the DNS records at your domain registrar.

How to Change the Nameservers with Different Registrars

If you're using a third-party DNS service (e.g., Cloudflare, Google DNS), you need to change the nameservers. Here's how you can do that with popular domain registrars:

GoDaddy:

Log in to your GoDaddy account.

Go to **"My Products"** and click on **"Domains"**.

Find the domain you want to update and click on **"DNS"** or **"Manage DNS"** next to the domain name.

Scroll down to the **"Nameservers"** section.

Click **"Change"** next to the current nameservers.

Choose **"Custom"** and enter your desired nameservers (e.g., ns1.example.com, ns2.example.com).

Click **"Save"** to apply the changes.

Wait for DNS propagation, which can take up to **48 hours**.

Namecheap:

Log in to your Namecheap account.

Go to **"Domain List"** and click on **"Manage"** next to the domain you want to modify.

Navigate to the **"Nameservers"** section.

Choose **"Custom DNS"** from the dropdown menu.

Enter your custom nameservers (e.g., ns1.example.com, ns2.example.com).

Click the checkmark to save the changes.

Wait for DNS propagation, which may take anywhere from a few minutes to 48 hours.

Google Domains:

Log in to your Google Domains account.

Select the domain you wish to change the nameservers for.

In the left-hand menu, click on "DNS".

Under the "Name servers" section, click "Use custom name servers".

Enter your custom nameservers (e.g., ns1.example.com, ns2.example.com).

Click "Save" to apply the changes.

Wait for DNS propagation, which may take anywhere from a few minutes to 48 hours.

Important Note:

If you don't need to use a third-party DNS provider and are simply pointing your domain to your server's static IP, you do not need to change your nameservers. Instead, modify the A record (Host record) in the DNS management section.

Adding MX(Mail Exchange) Records for Your Email Server

If you're setting up an email server, you will need to configure your domain's MX (Mail Exchange) records to handle email traffic. MX records tell the internet where to send email for your domain.

Steps for Adding MX Records with Your New Domain Name (e.g., mail.example.com) for Different Registrars:

GoDaddy:

Log in to your GoDaddy account.

Go to "My Products" and click on "Domains".

Find your domain and click on "DNS" or "Manage DNS" next to the domain name.

In the DNS Management section, click "Add" to add a new record.

For **Type**, select MX.

For **Host**, enter @ (to represent your root domain, e.g., example.com).

For **Points to**, enter your mail server's domain name (e.g., mail.example.com).

Set **Priority** (e.g., 10).

Set **TTL** to default or 1 hour.

Save changes and wait for propagation.

Namecheap:

Log in to your Namecheap account.

Go to "Domain List" and click on "Manage" next to the domain.

Navigate to the "Advanced DNS" tab.

Scroll to "Mail Settings" and click "Add New Record".

For **Type**, select MX.

For **Host**, enter @.

For **Value**, enter your mail server's domain name (e.g., mail.example.com).

Set **Priority** (e.g., 10).

Set **TTL** to default.

Save the changes.

Google Domains:

Log in to your Google Domains account.

Select the domain you want to manage.

Go to the "DNS" section.

Under "Custom resource records", click "Add".

For **Type**, select MX.

For **Host**, enter @.

For **Value**, enter your mail server's domain name (e.g., mail.example.com).

Set **Priority** (e.g., 10).

Set **TTL** to default (1 hour).

Click "Add" and save the changes.

Details of Your Domain Name for your Linux Server Configuration

A domain name consists of a Top-Level Domain (TLD) and a Second-Level Domain (SLD).

In *example.com*, **".com"** is the **Top-Level Domain (TLD)**.

In *example.com*, **"example"** is the **Second-Level Domain (SLD)**.

The hostname specifically identifies a particular service or server within a domain. The hostname can include a subdomain and the domain name itself (e.g., *www.example.com* or *mail.example.com*).

In these examples:

"www" is the **hostname** in *www.example.com*.

"mail" is the **hostname** in *mail.example.com*.

The full address *www.example.com* consists of:

The **hostname** ("www").

The **domain name** ("example.com").

The hostname indicates which specific server or service is being accessed within the domain.

Fully Qualified Domain Name (FQDN) – Required for certain server configurations, including email servers, to ensure proper identification and routing of services on the internet.

A Fully Qualified Domain Name (FQDN) includes:

The **hostname** (e.g., "www" or "mail").

The **domain name** (e.g., "example.com").

Optionally, a **trailing dot** to signify the root domain (e.g., "www.example.com.").

The FQDN fully specifies the address, leaving no ambiguity about the server or service being accessed.

In most cases, when no subdomain is specified, the domain name itself can also act as the hostname.

Web Hosting Essentials (Dynamic IP)

Next, we'll dive into the essentials of web hosting—understanding the role of domains and DNS (Domain Name System). A domain is the address users type into their browsers to access your website, while DNS translates domain names into IP addresses that servers use to communicate. In this section, we'll explain how to register a domain and configure it to point to your server.

Registering a Domain Name and Pointing it to your Linux Server for Dynamic IP

Your IP address is assigned by your ISP. If your Linux server has a dynamic IP address, it means the IP can change periodically. Dynamic IPs are generally more affordable and are typically considered home-level connections by most ISPs. This requires a slightly different approach for configuring your domain.

Choose a Domain Name

Brainstorm: Think about what you want your domain name to represent. It should be short, memorable, and relevant to your website's purpose.

Consider Keywords: If applicable, try to include relevant keywords that relate to your business or personal brand.

Check Availability: Use a domain name checker tool (most domain registrars have one) to check if the domain name you want is available.

Select a Domain Registrar

A domain registrar is a company authorized to sell domain names.

Popular registrars include:

GoDaddy - https://www.godaddy.com/

Namecheap - https://www.namecheap.com/

Google Domains - https://domains.google/

Search for Your Domain Name

Go to the registrar's website.

Enter the domain name you want to register into the search bar.

The registrar will tell you if the domain is available or not. If

it's taken, you may need to try a different name or a different TLD (e.g., .com, .org, .net, .biz).

Select Your Domain Name and TLD

Choose a TLD: TLD stands for Top-Level Domain (like .com, .net, .org, .co, etc.).

Consider Alternatives: If your first choice isn't available, you can try using a different TLD or slightly modify the domain name to find an available option. You can also select a TLD that signifies your country, such as (.us for the USA, .ca for Canada, .uk for the UK, etc.).

Add Domain Privacy Protection (Optional)

Many registrars offer WHOIS protection or Domain Privacy Protection, which keeps your personal information (such as your address and phone number) private in the public WHOIS database. This is a useful feature, as it helps protect you from being inundated with unsolicited business offers. This is optional but recommended to protect your privacy.

Create an Account with the Registrar

If you don't already have an account with the registrar, you'll need to create one.

This involves entering your personal details and setting up a payment method.

Add Your Domain to the Cart and Proceed to Checkout

Once you've selected your domain, you can proceed to checkout.

Most registrars offer domain registration for one year, with the option to extend the registration for multiple years.

Complete the Purchase

Provide your billing information and confirm the purchase. After completing the payment, you will have successfully registered your domain!

Verify Your Registration

After registration, the registrar will usually send you an email to verify your domain name registration. Be sure to confirm it. You will also be listed as the domain owner in the WHOIS database.

Renew Your Domain

Domains typically need to be renewed annually. Keep track of your renewal dates to ensure you don't lose ownership of your domain.

Point Your New Domain to Your Linux Server with a Dynamic IP Address Using DDNS

If your Linux server has a dynamic IP address, the IP may change over time. You will need to use Dynamic DNS (DDNS). Dynamic DNS can automatically update your domain's DNS records with your current IP address each time it changes, allowing you to maintain reliable access to your server.

When you have a dynamic IP address on your Linux server, and you want to use your own domain name (e.g., yourdomain.com) instead of relying on a subdomain provided by a DDNS service (e.g., yourdomain.no-ip.org), you'll need to follow a few steps to configure DDNS with your own domain.

Here's a step-by-step guide to set this up.

Step 1: Set Up a DDNS Provider

You'll need to sign up with a DDNS provider, which will automatically update your domain's DNS records when your dynamic IP address changes. Some popular DDNS services include:

Steps to Set Up DDNS with Your Own Domain:

Sign Up for a DDNS Service: First, you'll need to choose a **DDNS service that allows custom domain names**.

Some popular DDNS providers that offer this feature include:

Dynu

No-IP

DuckDNS

Create an account with one of these providers. For this example, we will use No-IP and follow their setup process. You'll typically be asked to choose a subdomain (e.g., yourdomain.no-ip.org) as part of the registration.

Configure DDNS on Your Linux Server: After signing up for a DDNS service, you'll be given a client (software or script) that needs to run on your server. This client will automatically update your domain's DNS records with the current dynamic IP. Follow the provider's instructions to install and configure the DDNS client on your server.

Here's an example with No-IP:

Install the No-IP DUC (Dynamic Update Client) on your Linux server.

Run the client to keep your IP address updated.

The client will need to be configured to update your DDNS service provider with the correct IP.

Update DNS Records with Your Custom Domain: Now that you have a DDNS service updating your IP, the next step is to configure your domain registrar (e.g., GoDaddy, Namecheap, or Google Domains) to point to your dynamic IP using your custom domain.

Log in to your domain registrar and go to the **DNS Management** section for your domain.

Add an **A Record** (Host Record) that points to the IP provided by your DDNS service. If you're using a provider like **No-IP**, they may also give you a hostname (e.g., yoursdomain.no-ip.org).

For example:

Host: @ (represents your root domain, e.g., yourdomain.com)

Points To: yourdomain.no-ip.org (or whatever your DDNS hostname is)

TTL: Set to a default value (e.g., 1 hour)

Configure Subdomains or Other Records (if needed): If you're using subdomains (e.g., mail.yourdomain.com or www.yourdomain.com), create additional A or CNAME

records to point them to the dynamic IP or DDNS hostname, depending on your configuration.

For example:

Host: www

Points To: yourdomain.no-ip.org

Test Your Setup: After configuring the DNS records, allow some time for DNS propagation. Test your domain by typing it into a browser or using tools like ping or nslookup to ensure it's resolving correctly.

If everything is set up correctly, your dynamic IP will now be associated with your custom domain name, and you'll be able to access your server reliably, even as your IP changes.

Important Notes:

DDNS services typically update your DNS records at regular intervals or when a change is detected. Some services provide a feature to update more frequently if your IP changes often.

Make sure to keep the DDNS client running on your Linux server to ensure that your IP is always updated in the DNS records.

Setting up a DDNS Client so Your Linux Server will work with Pointing to your changing IP

You will need to set up a DDNS (Dynamic DNS) client on your Linux server if you want the dynamic IP address to be automatically updated with your DDNS provider whenever it changes. The DDNS client communicates with your DDNS provider to notify them of any IP changes, ensuring your domain always points to the correct address.

Choose a DDNS Provider

Select a DDNS provider that supports custom domain

names. Popular services include:

Dynu

No-IP

DuckDNS

Many of these services offer free or paid plans with the ability to use your own domain.

Install the DDNS Client on Your Linux Server:

Once you've signed up for a DDNS service, you'll typically need to install the DDNS update client software on your

Linux server. The client will regularly check your server's current IP and update your DDNS provider with the new IP when it changes.

For example, here's how you would set up the No-IP client:

Install No-IP Client on Linux - Download and Install the No-IP DUC (Dynamic Update Client)

Run the following commands to install the No-IP client on a Debian-based system (e.g., Ubuntu):

sudo apt-get update

sudo apt-get install build-essential

```
wget http://www.no-ip.org/client/linux/noip-duc-linux.tar.gz
```

```
tar xf noip-duc-linux.tar.gz
cd noip-2.1.9-1
sudo make
sudo make install
```

Configure the No-IP Client:

After installing, configure the client with your No-IP credentials:

```
sudo /usr/local/bin/noip2 -C
```

This command will prompt you to enter your No-IP username, password, and the hostname you want to use (e.g., yourserver.no-ip.org).

Start the No-IP Service:

To ensure that the DDNS client runs in the background and updates your IP address automatically, start the service with:

```
sudo /usr/local/bin/noip2
```

You can also set it to start automatically when your server

boots by adding it to the startup scripts or using systemd.

For example, to add it to systemd, create a service file:

sudo nano /etc/systemd/system/noip2.service

Add the following content to the service file:

```
[Unit]
Description=No-IP DUC Client
After=network.target

[Service]
ExecStart=/usr/local/bin/noip2
Restart=always
User=root

[Install]
WantedBy=multi-user.target
```
Save the file, then reload systemd and enable the service:
bash
Copy code
```
sudo systemctl daemon-reload
sudo systemctl enable noip2
sudo systemctl start noip2
```

Check if It's Working: You can verify that the client is running and updating your IP with the following command:

sudo /usr/local/bin/noip2 -S

This will display the current IP address the DDNS service is using.

Point Your Domain to the Dynamic IP:

After setting up the DDNS client, you need to configure your domain registrar to point your domain to your DDNS hostname.

Login to your domain registrar (e.g., GoDaddy, Namecheap, Google Domains).

Go to the DNS management section for your domain.

Create an A record (or modify an existing one) that points to your DDNS hostname (e.g., yourdomain.no-ip.org).

Host: @ (for the root domain)

Points To: yourdomain.no-ip.org (or the equivalent hostname provided by your DDNS service)

TTL: You can set this to the default (e.g., 1 hour).

Test the Setup:

Once everything is configured, test your domain by accessing it via a browser or using tools like ping or nslookup. Ensure it resolves to the correct dynamic IP.

Why Do You Need the DDNS Client?

The DDNS client is crucial because it automates the process of updating the DNS records with the current IP address. Without it, you would need to manually update your domain's A record every time your IP address changes, which is time-consuming and impractical. The client ensures that your domain name always points to the correct dynamic IP, even if it changes periodically.

Setting up a DDNS client on your Linux server is necessary if you want to use your own domain with a dynamic IP address. The client will automatically keep your DNS records updated with the correct IP, ensuring that you can always access your server using your domain name.

Enabling Linux Server Access to the Internet & Firewall Hardening Basics

When setting up a Linux server to host your website, email, FTP, and SSH services, configuring a firewall is one of the first and most critical steps. A properly configured firewall ensures that only necessary services are accessible, while blocking potential threats and malicious attacks.

Security is a top priority when hosting a server. In this section, we'll guide you through the process of server hardening—the essential practice of securing your server against unauthorized access, attacks, and vulnerabilities.

We'll cover the basics of configuring a firewall, specifically using UFW (Uncomplicated Firewall), to control the incoming and outgoing traffic on your server. Additionally, we'll discuss best practices for maintaining your server's security, including applying regular security updates and patches.

We'll also provide key guidelines for **SSH security**, such as disabling root login, implementing key-based authentication, and enforcing strong password policies to prevent unauthorized access to your server.

Here's how you can set up UFW (Uncomplicated Firewall) for a web server, email server, FTP server, and SSH on your Linux server. This guide also includes best practices for server hardening to secure your server.

Install UFW (Uncomplicated Firewall)

First, ensure that UFW is installed on your system. If it isn't, you can install it using:

sudo apt update

sudo apt install ufw

Basic UFW Configuration for Web Server, Email Server, FTP Server, and SSH

Once UFW is installed, you need to configure it to allow traffic for the services your server will host (web, email, FTP, and SSH). You'll also block any unnecessary ports to secure your server.

Allow SSH Traffic (Port 22)

SSH is essential for managing your server remotely, but it is critical to secure it. Before enabling UFW, allow SSH traffic to ensure you don't lock yourself out of the server.

sudo ufw allow ssh

This rule allows inbound traffic on port 22, which is the default port for SSH.

Best Practice for SSH Security

Disable root login: To prevent unauthorized root login attempts, edit the SSH config file (/etc/ssh/sshd_config) and set PermitRootLogin to no:

sudo nano /etc/ssh/sshd_config

Find the line that says PermitRootLogin and change it to:

PermitRootLogin no

Use SSH Key-based Authentication: Generate an SSH key pair and add your public key to ~/.ssh/authorized_keys on the server. Disable password authentication:

```
sudo nano /etc/ssh/sshd_config
```

Set:

```
PasswordAuthentication no
```

After making these changes, restart SSH:

```
sudo systemctl restart ssh
```

Allow Web Traffic (HTTP/HTTPS) (Ports 80 and 443)

If you're running a web server (e.g., Apache, Nginx), you'll need to allow HTTP (port 80) and HTTPS (port 443) traffic.

```
sudo ufw allow http
sudo ufw allow https
```

Or, you can explicitly allow ports 80 and 443:

```
sudo ufw allow 80,443/tcp
```

Allow Email Server Traffic (SMTP, IMAP, and POP3)

If you have an email server running (e.g., Postfix, Dovecot), you'll need to allow email protocols like SMTP (port 25), IMAP (port 143), IMAPS (port 993), and POP3 (port 110).

For SMTP, IMAP, and POP3, allow the necessary ports:

sudo ufw allow smtp

sudo ufw allow imap

sudo ufw allow pop3

For IMAPS (secure IMAP) and POP3S (secure POP3):

sudo ufw allow imaps

sudo ufw allow pop3s

Allow FTP Traffic (Port 21 and Passive Ports)

If you're running an FTP server (e.g., vsftpd), you'll need to allow FTP traffic on port 21.

sudo ufw allow ftp

Additionally, FTP requires a range of **passive ports** for data transfer. You may need to configure your FTP server to use a specific range of ports and then allow them through UFW.

For example, if you configure FTP to use ports 50000-51000:

sudo ufw allow 50000:51000/tcp

Enable UFW

After configuring UFW with the necessary rules, enable the firewall.

sudo ufw enable

You'll be prompted to confirm that you want to enable the firewall. Type y and hit Enter.

Check UFW Status and Rules

To ensure that UFW is running and your rules are in place, you can check the status with:

sudo ufw status verbose

This will display a list of all allowed and denied services, showing the ports and protocols.

Monitor and Apply Security Updates Regularly

To keep your server secure, it's important to install security updates and patches regularly. You can enable automatic updates for security patches by configuring the unattended-upgrades package.

First, install it:

sudo apt install unattended-upgrades

Then, configure automatic updates:

sudo dpkg-reconfigure --priority=low unattended-upgrades

This will enable your system to automatically install security updates.

Best Practices for Server Hardening

In addition to setting up the firewall, there are other key security best practices you should follow:

Keep your system updated: Always keep your system and software up to date to mitigate known vulnerabilities.

sudo apt update && sudo apt upgrade

Disable unused services: Disable services you don't need to reduce the attack surface of your server. For example, you can disable FTP if you're not using it:

```
sudo systemctl disable vsftpd
```

Use Fail2ban: Fail2ban can help protect your server from brute-force attacks by blocking IPs that make too many failed login attempts. Install it:

```
sudo apt install fail2ban
```

Limit login attempts: Configure login policies to prevent brute-force attacks by limiting the number of login attempts.

Disable Unnecessary Ports

Once your firewall is configured, it's a good practice to ensure that only the necessary ports are open. You can use the following command to block all incoming traffic except the ones you've allowed:

```
sudo ufw default deny incoming
sudo ufw default allow outgoing
```

Final Check

After applying these configurations, your server should be secure and hardened. To check the status of your firewall:

```
sudo ufw status verbose
```

You should see something similar to:

Status: active

To	Action	From
--	------	----
22	ALLOW	Anywhere
80	ALLOW	Anywhere
443	ALLOW	Anywhere
25	ALLOW	Anywhere
110	ALLOW	Anywhere
143	ALLOW	Anywhere
993	ALLOW	Anywhere
21	ALLOW	Anywhere
50000:51000/tcp	ALLOW	Anywhere
22 (v6)	ALLOW	Anywhere (v6)
80 (v6)	ALLOW	Anywhere (v6)
443 (v6)	ALLOW	Anywhere (v6)
25 (v6)	ALLOW	Anywhere (v6)
110 (v6)	ALLOW	Anywhere (v6)
143 (v6)	ALLOW	Anywhere (v6)
993 (v6)	ALLOW	Anywhere (v6)
21 (v6)	ALLOW	Anywhere (v6)
50000:51000/tcp (v6)	ALLOW	Anywhere (v6)

This shows that the necessary ports are open, and the firewall is properly configured.

By following these steps, you will have a secure, hardened server with an active firewall that only allows the traffic necessary for your web, email, FTP, and SSH services.

Chapter 3: Setting Up Your Email Server (Static or Dynamic IP)

Why Set Up Your Own Email Server?

In this chapter, we delve into the advantages and considerations of running your own email server versus using third-party services like Gmail, Yahoo, or Outlook. While third-party providers offer convenience and reliable service, hosting your own email server provides greater control, enhanced privacy, and more customization options. With your own server, you can manage your domain, create custom email addresses, and ensure that your data remains private.

However, running an email server comes with its own challenges, such as ensuring uptime, managing spam, and maintaining security. We'll carefully examine the benefits—

control, privacy, and custom domains—alongside the challenges—maintenance, security, and deliverability—to help you make an informed decision about whether hosting your own email server is right for you.

Although it's possible to configure an email server with both static and dynamic IP addresses, we will emphasize the advantages of setting up email servers with a static IP for

optimal performance. For users with dynamic IPs, many reliable third-party email service providers offer excellent solutions at reasonable costs, making them a viable alternative.

This chapter will also provide you with step-by-step instructions for installing Postfix, Dovecot, and SpamAssassin, whether you're using a static or dynamic IP. By the end, you'll have a fully functional email server up and running.

Installing and Configuring Postfix (SMTP Server)

The heart of sending and receiving emails on your server lies in the Postfix mail transfer agent (MTA). In this section, we guide you through the installation and configuration of Postfix, which will handle your outgoing emails (SMTP).

Postfix Setup: First, we'll install Postfix using your Linux distribution's package manager, and then we'll walk you through configuring basic SMTP settings such as the server's hostname and domain name.

Configuring Postfix: Next, we'll set up secure email sending by configuring Postfix to support encrypted connections (via TLS) and authentication mechanisms to prevent

unauthorized email sending. This step ensures your emails are transmitted securely over the internet.

Virtual Mailboxes: Postfix also needs to know how to handle incoming mail for different users. We'll show you how to create virtual mailboxes for user accounts, allowing you to handle both incoming and outgoing emails for each user on your domain. This setup will enable you to manage multiple email addresses efficiently.

Install & Configure Your Email Server with a Static IP

Below is a step-by-step guide for installing and configuring Postfix (an SMTP server) on a Linux server with a static IP:

Update Your System

Before starting with Postfix installation, make sure your server is up to date by running the following commands:

```
sudo apt update

sudo apt upgrade -y
```

This ensures that your system is up-to-date with the latest security patches.

Install Postfix

Postfix is available in most Linux distributions' default repositories. To install it, run the following command:

```
sudo apt install postfix -y
```

During installation, you will be prompted to configure the mail server. You can choose the appropriate configuration option based on your needs. For a simple static IP setup, you can choose **Internet Site**.

Configure Postfix

Once Postfix is installed, we will need to configure it for use with your static IP.

Edit the Postfix Main Configuration File:

The main configuration file for Postfix is located at /etc/postfix/main.cf.

Open it for editing with the following command:

```
sudo nano /etc/postfix/main.cf
```

Key Configuration Settings

Make sure the following lines are present in the main.cf file:

```
# Replace with your domain name
myhostname = mail.yourdomain.com

# Replace with your domain name
mydomain = yourdomain.com

myorigin = /etc/mailname

# Allows listening on all interfaces (can be 'loopback-only' if
# you want it restricted)
inet_interfaces = all

# To restrict Postfix to IPv4 if necessary
inet_protocols = ipv4
mydestination = $myhostname, localhost.$mydomain, localhost,
$mydomain
mynetworks = 127.0.0.0/8, [::1]/128   # Only local networks and
localhost

# Mail storage directory
home_mailbox = Maildir/
```

myhostname: Set this to your fully qualified domain name (FQDN).

mydomain: Your domain name (e.g., example.com).

inet_interfaces: Set to all to accept mail on all network interfaces. You can change this to loopback-only if you're only sending mail from localhost.

mynetworks: Defines the networks Postfix will relay mail from. Here, it's configured to allow mail from localhost.

home_mailbox: The location where mail will be stored, in this case, the Maildir/ directory.

Set up DNS and MX Record:

You must ensure that your domain's **MX record** points to your server's IP address (the static IP you've assigned). The **MX record** should be set up in your domain's DNS settings (this is usually done through your domain registrar's website).

Example for MX record:

@ IN MX 10 mail.yourdomain.com.

This tells the world that your mail server (Postfix) is located at mail.yourdomain.com.

Set up the Mailbox Format

Postfix uses a directory structure to store emails. It's common to use **Maildir** format, which is preferred for performance reasons.

Create a Maildir directory for the user that will receive emails:

sudo mkdir -p /home/youruser/Maildir

sudo chown -R youruser:youruser /home/youruser/Maildir

If you're configuring Postfix to use a specific user, make sure the directory has the correct permissions.

Configure Postfix to Send Mail Relaying

For external email delivery, you may need to configure Postfix to send mail through a relay server (e.g., if you're not directly connected to the internet or have an external SMTP server). This is optional for simple setups with static IPs.

To use an external SMTP relay:

sudo nano /etc/postfix/sasl_passwd

In this file, add the relay server login information:

[smtp.relayserver.com]:587   username:password

Then, secure this file and map it to Postfix:

sudo postmap /etc/postfix/sasl_passwd

sudo chmod 600 /etc/postfix/sasl_passwd

Now, edit the Postfix main configuration file again to tell it to use this relay:

sudo nano /etc/postfix/main.cf

Add the following lines:

```
# Your SMTP relay server
relayhost = [smtp.relayserver.com]:587

smtp_sasl_auth_enable = yes
smtp_sasl_password_maps = hash:/etc/postfix/sasl_passwd
smtp_sasl_security_options = noanonymous
```

This configuration will authenticate Postfix with the SMTP relay using the credentials in sasl_passwd.

Restart Postfix

Once the configuration is complete, restart Postfix to apply the changes:

```
sudo systemctl restart postfix
```

Test the Postfix Configuration

You can test your mail server by sending a test email:

```
echo "Test email body" | mail -s "Test Email Subject" recipient@example.com
```

This will send a test email. Check your inbox to verify that the email was successfully delivered.

To troubleshoot and see if there are any issues with the configuration, you can check the Postfix logs:

sudo tail -f /var/log/mail.log

Allow Postfix Through the Firewall

If you are using a firewall (e.g., UFW), make sure to allow traffic on port 25 (SMTP):

sudo ufw allow 25

If you're using iptables:

sudo iptables -A INPUT -p tcp --dport 25 -j ACCEPT

Set Up SSL/TLS (Optional, for Secure Email Transmission)

For secure email transmission (SSL/TLS), you can enable encryption in Postfix. To use **STARTTLS**, make sure your Postfix configuration includes the following lines in the main.cf:

smtpd_use_tls = yes

smtpd_tls_cert_file = /etc/ssl/certs/yourdomain.com.crt

smtpd_tls_key_file = /etc/ssl/private/yourdomain.com.key

Make sure to replace the file paths with the actual paths to your SSL certificate and private key.

Install & Configure Your Email Server with a Dynamic IP

Below is a step-by-step guide for installing and configuring Postfix (an SMTP server) on a Linux server with a dynamic IP (e.g., yourdomain.no-ip.org). You will need a paid No-IP account with a custom domain, which resolves yourdomain.no-ip.org to your actual domain (e.g., yourdomain.com) in order to properly set up the email server.

Update Your System

Before installing Postfix, update your system to ensure all packages are up-to-date.

sudo apt update

sudo apt upgrade -y

Install Postfix

Postfix is available in most Linux distributions' default repositories. To install Postfix on your system, use the following command:

sudo apt install postfix -y

During the installation process, you'll be prompted with the Postfix configuration screen. For a dynamic IP setup, select Internet Site when prompted, and set your hostname to your No-IP domain name (e.g., yourdomain.no-ip.org).

If you skip this during installation, you can later configure Postfix manually by editing the main configuration file.

Configure Postfix

Once Postfix is installed, it must be configured for use with your dynamic IP setup. The key configuration changes will revolve around your dynamic domain name and ensuring that mail can be sent and received despite the IP changing.

Edit the Postfix Main Configuration File

Open the main.cf configuration file for editing:

sudo nano /etc/postfix/main.cf

Key Configuration Settings:

myhostname: Set this to your dynamic DNS hostname (e.g., yourdomain.no-ip.org).

mydomain: Set this to your domain name (e.g., yourdomain.com).

myorigin: Set this to your domain, or use /etc/mailname (default).

inet_interfaces: Set to all so that Postfix listens on all network interfaces, or loopback-only if you only want local mail.

inet_protocols: Set this to ipv4 to restrict Postfix to only use IPv4.

Here is an example of the key configuration values:

```
# Your dynamic DNS hostname
myhostname = yourdomain.no-ip.org

# Your domain name
mydomain = yourdomain.com
myorigin = /etc/mailname

# Listen on all interfaces
inet_interfaces = all

# Use IPv4 for SMTP
inet_protocols = ipv4
mydestination = $myhostname, localhost.$mydomain, localhost, $mydomain

# Only allow local networks and localhost
mynetworks = 127.0.0.0/8, [::1]/128

# Mailbox directory for users
home_mailbox = Maildir/
```

DNS and MX Record Configuration:

With a dynamic IP, you'll need to ensure that your No-IP service is keeping your domain's MX record updated to point to your server's public IP. No-IP can automatically update the A record (your IP address) each time it changes.

Ensure that your MX record in the DNS settings (on No-IP or your domain registrar) points to your dynamic domain (e.g., yourdomain.no-ip.org).

Example for MX record:

@ IN MX 10 yourdomain.no-ip.org.

Configure Dynamic DNS with No-IP

If you haven't already set up a dynamic DNS service with No-IP, follow these steps to install and configure their dynamic IP updater on your server:

Install the No-IP Dynamic Update Client

Download and install the No-IP client to update your dynamic IP:

sudo apt install make gcc

```
wget https://www.no-ip.org/client/linux/noip-duc-linux.tar.gz
```

```
tar xzf noip-duc-linux.tar.gz
```

```
cd noip-2.1.9-1/
```

```
sudo make
```

```
sudo make install
```

Set Up the No-IP Client:

After installation, run the No-IP client configuration:

```
sudo /usr/local/bin/noip2 -C
```

Follow the prompts to set up your No-IP account and specify the domain you created (e.g., yourdomain.no-ip.org).

Start the No-IP Service:

Start the No-IP service to update your dynamic IP address:

```
sudo /usr/local/bin/noip2
```

You can set No-IP to start automatically on boot:

```
sudo systemctl enable noip2
```

Verify No-IP Update:

To check if No-IP is correctly updating your IP address:

/usr/local/bin/noip2 -S

Configure Postfix to Use a Relay Server (Optional but Recommended)

If you are using a dynamic IP, many ISPs block outgoing mail on port 25 to prevent spam. This means you'll need to relay mail through an external SMTP server. Here's how you can configure Postfix to use a relay server (e.g., Gmail, SendGrid, etc.).

Create a SASL Password File:

To relay mail through an external SMTP server, you need to configure SMTP authentication.

sudo nano /etc/postfix/sasl_passwd

Add the following:

[smtp.gmail.com]:587   your-email@gmail.com:yourpassword

Secure the Password File

Set the correct permissions:

sudo postmap /etc/postfix/sasl_passwd

sudo chmod 600 /etc/postfix/sasl_passwd

Update Postfix Configuration to Use the Relay

Open the main.cf file again:

sudo nano /etc/postfix/main.cf

Add or modify the following lines:

relayhost = [smtp.gmail.com]:587 # Use your relay server's SMTP settings

smtp_sasl_auth_enable = yes

smtp_sasl_password_maps = hash:/etc/postfix/sasl_passwd

smtp_sasl_security_options = noanonymous

Restart Postfix

After making these changes, restart Postfix:

sudo systemctl restart postfix

Test Your Email Server

Now that Postfix is installed and configured, you should test your server to ensure that it can send and receive email.

You can send a test email using the mail command:

echo "Test email body" | mail -s "Test Email Subject" recipient@example.com

Check the recipient's inbox to see if the email was received. **You can also check the Postfix log for any errors:**

sudo tail -f /var/log/mail.log

Configure the Firewall (if applicable)

If you are using a firewall, make sure to allow SMTP traffic (port 25) through your firewall:

UFW:

sudo ufw allow 25

iptables:

sudo iptables -A INPUT -p tcp --dport 25 -j ACCEPT

SSL/TLS for Secure Email Transmission (Optional)

For secure email communication, you should configure **SSL/TLS** for Postfix.

Generate SSL Certificates (or obtain them from a trusted certificate authority):

You can generate a self-signed certificate (not recommended for production):

sudo mkdir -p /etc/ssl/certs

sudo mkdir -p /etc/ssl/private

sudo openssl req -new -x509 -days 365 -nodes -out /etc/ssl/certs/mail.yourdomain.crt -keyout /etc/ssl/private/mail.yourdomain.key

Configure Postfix to Use SSL/TLS:

Edit /etc/postfix/main.cf:

smtpd_use_tls = yes

smtpd_tls_cert_file = /etc/ssl/certs/mail.yourdomain.crt

smtpd_tls_key_file = /etc/ssl/private/mail.yourdomain.key

Restart Postfix:

sudo systemctl restart postfix

Setting Up Dovecot for IMAP and POP3

While Postfix takes care of sending emails, Dovecot is responsible for handling the retrieval of emails on the server. Dovecot is a widely used IMAP and POP3 server that provides a means for users to access their email accounts from various devices.

Installing Dovecot: We'll walk you through the installation of Dovecot and its integration with Postfix to handle the reception of emails.

Securing Email Communication: To ensure that your emails are transmitted securely, we'll enable SSL/TLS encryption for both incoming (IMAP/POP3) and outgoing (SMTP) email traffic. This step ensures that sensitive email content is encrypted in transit, providing privacy and protection against eavesdropping.

Testing Email Sending and Receiving: After configuration, we'll guide you through sending test emails using Postfix and receiving them via Dovecot, confirming that the system is set up correctly and both inbound and outbound email are functioning as expected.

Install & Configure Dovecot with Static IP

First, install Dovecot using your package manager.

For **Debian/Ubuntu**:

sudo apt update

sudo apt install dovecot-core dovecot-imapd dovecot-pop3d

For **CentOS/RHEL**:

sudo yum install dovecot

For **Fedora**:

sudo dnf install dovecot

Step 2: Configure Dovecot for Static IP

Now, configure Dovecot to allow email access via IMAP/POP3.

Open the main Dovecot configuration file:

sudo nano /etc/dovecot/dovecot.conf

Ensure the following basic settings are in place:

Set the hostname to your server's domain (or IP address if using without DNS):

host = yourdomain.com # or use your static IP if necessary

Enable IMAP and/or POP3 depending on your needs:

protocols = imap pop3

If you are using SSL/TLS encryption (which is highly recommended), ensure Dovecot is set up to use secure connections:

ssl = required

ssl_cert = </etc/ssl/certs/yourdomain.crt

ssl_key = </etc/ssl/private/yourdomain.key

Replace yourdomain.crt and yourdomain.key with the correct paths to your SSL certificate and private key files.

You may also need to configure authentication settings depending on how you plan to authenticate users. You can use system user accounts or configure a virtual user setup (e.g., using MySQL, PostgreSQL).

For local user authentication:

auth_mechanisms = plain login

Step 3: Configure Mailboxes and Directories

Dovecot stores emails in mailboxes. The default mailbox format is typically **Maildir**. Here's how to configure it:

Open the file where you define mailbox storage options:

sudo nano /etc/dovecot/conf.d/10-mail.conf

Find and modify the following lines:

Enable Maildir storage:

mail_location = maildir:~/Maildir

Set the user and group for mail storage:

mail_uid = vmail

mail_gid = vmail

Step 4: Set Permissions for Mail Directory

Set the correct permissions for the mail directory to ensure Dovecot can access the user's mail:

sudo mkdir -p /home/user/Maildir

sudo chown -R user:vmail /home/user/Maildir

sudo chmod -R 700 /home/user/Maildir

Step 5: Start Dovecot

Once the configuration is complete, restart the Dovecot service to apply the changes:

For **Debian/Ubuntu**:

sudo systemctl restart dovecot

For **CentOS/RHEL/Fedora**:

sudo systemctl restart dovecot

Step 6: Enable Dovecot to Start on Boot

To ensure Dovecot starts automatically upon server boot, enable it:

sudo systemctl enable dovecot

Step 7: Test Dovecot Configuration

To ensure everything is configured correctly, use the following command to check Dovecot's status:

```
sudo systemctl status dovecot
```

If everything is set up correctly, you should see a status message indicating that Dovecot is active and running.

Step 8: Test Email Connectivity

Use telnet or openssl to test the IMAP or POP3 service:

For IMAP:

```
telnet yourdomain.com 143
```

For IMAPS (secure IMAP):

```
openssl s_client -connect yourdomain.com:993
```

For POP3:

```
telnet yourdomain.com 110
```

For POP3S (secure POP3):

```
openssl s_client -connect yourdomain.com:995
```

Step 9: Configure Firewall (if applicable)

If your server has a firewall enabled, ensure that the necessary ports for IMAP, IMAPS, POP3, and POP3S are open. The typical ports are:

IMAP: 143

IMAPS (Secure IMAP): 993

POP3: 110

POP3S (Secure POP3): 995

For UFW (Ubuntu/Debian-based systems), run the following commands:

sudo ufw allow 143/tcp

sudo ufw allow 993/tcp

sudo ufw allow 110/tcp

sudo ufw allow 995/tcp

For firewalld (CentOS/RHEL-based systems), use the following:

sudo firewall-cmd --permanent --add-port=143/tcp

sudo firewall-cmd --permanent --add-port=993/tcp

sudo firewall-cmd --permanent --add-port=110/tcp

sudo firewall-cmd --permanent --add-port=995/tcp

```
sudo firewall-cmd --reload
```

Install & Configure Dovecot with Dynamic IP

Install Dovecot

To begin, install Dovecot using your Linux distribution's package manager.

For **Debian/Ubuntu**:

```
sudo apt update
sudo apt install dovecot-core dovecot-imapd dovecot-pop3d
```

For **CentOS/RHEL**:

```
sudo yum install dovecot
```

For **Fedora**:

```
sudo dnf install dovecot
```

Step 2: Configure Dovecot for Dynamic IP

Since you're using a **dynamic IP** with a service like **No-IP**, you will need to configure Dovecot with the correct domain name, which is updated by your dynamic DNS service.

Open the main Dovecot configuration file:

```
sudo nano /etc/dovecot/dovecot.conf
```

Update the host setting to your dynamic DNS domain (e.g., yourdomain.no-ip.org):

```
# Use the dynamic DNS hostname

host = yourdomain.no-ip.org
```

Enable IMAP and/or POP3 protocols, depending on which you want to support. Most email clients prefer IMAP for syncing emails across devices:

```
protocols = imap pop3
```

Configure SSL/TLS for encrypted email access (optional but recommended for secure communication). This requires an SSL certificate (either self-signed or from a trusted CA):

```
ssl = required

ssl_cert = </etc/ssl/certs/yourdomain.crt

ssl_key = </etc/ssl/private/yourdomain.key
```

Replace yourdomain.crt and yourdomain.key with the appropriate certificate and key files.

Step 3: Configure Mailboxes and Directories

Now, you will set up Dovecot to store email in Maildir format, which is common for modern email servers.

Edit the mail storage configuration:

sudo nano /etc/dovecot/conf.d/10-mail.conf

Configure the mail_location as Maildir:

mail_location = maildir:~/Maildir

Set the user and group for the mail storage directory:

mail_uid = vmail

mail_gid = vmail

Ensure that the mail directory exists for each user. You can create the Maildir structure manually if needed:

sudo mkdir -p /home/user/Maildir

sudo chown -R user:vmail /home/user/Maildir

sudo chmod -R 700 /home/user/Maildir

Step 4: Configure Authentication (Optional)

If you want to configure user authentication for Dovecot, you can set up a simple system user or virtual users using a database (such as MySQL or PostgreSQL). For now, let's configure Dovecot to use system authentication.

Open the authentication configuration file:

sudo nano /etc/dovecot/conf.d/10-auth.conf

Set the auth mechanism to plain login for basic username/password authentication:

auth_mechanisms = plain login

Make sure allow plaintext authentication is enabled for unencrypted logins (unless you're using SSL/TLS):

disable_plaintext_auth = no

Step 5: Start Dovecot

Once all configurations are complete, restart Dovecot to apply the changes.

For Debian/Ubuntu:

sudo systemctl restart dovecot

For CentOS/RHEL/Fedora:

sudo systemctl restart dovecot

Step 6: Enable Dovecot to Start on Boot

To ensure Dovecot starts automatically when the server reboots, run the following command:

sudo systemctl enable dovecot

Step 7: Test Dovecot Configuration

To check if Dovecot is running properly, you can verify its status:

sudo systemctl status dovecot

If everything is configured correctly, you should see a message indicating that Dovecot is active and running.

Step 8: Test Email Connectivity

Once Dovecot is running, test your email server's IMAP/POP3 functionality by connecting to it. You can use telnet or openssl for this.

For IMAP:

telnet yourdomain.no-ip.org 143

For IMAPS (secure IMAP):

openssl s_client -connect yourdomain.no-ip.org:993

For POP3:

telnet yourdomain.no-ip.org 110

For POP3S (secure POP3):

openssl s_client -connect yourdomain.no-ip.org:995

Step 9: Configure the Dynamic DNS Service (No-IP)

To keep your domain pointing to your dynamic IP address, you must configure the dynamic DNS service (e.g., No-IP).

Here's a brief guide:

Create an account at No-IP (if you don't have one already).

Add a **hostname** (e.g., yourdomain.no-ip.org).

Install the No-IP DUC (Dynamic Update Client) on your server to keep the IP address updated:

On Ubuntu/Debian:

sudo apt install noip2

On CentOS/RHEL:

sudo yum install noip

Configure the No-IP DUC to update your IP:

sudo noip2 -C

Follow the instructions to input your No-IP account credentials and configure the dynamic DNS service.

Add an MX Record for Your Dynamic IP with your Domain Registrar

Once logged in to your registrar, you can add the MX record that directs email traffic to your server.

Locate the DNS management settings for your domain. This may be listed as DNS Settings, DNS Management, Manage DNS, or something similar.

Add an MX record by following these steps:

Host: This is typically the part of the email address before the @ symbol. For example, if you want mail@yourdomain.com to point to your server, you would set the host to mail.

If you want the MX record to apply to your entire domain (i.e., yourdomain.com), set the host to @ (the "root" of the domain).

Value/Points To: This is where you specify the hostname that should receive the email. In your case, this will be your dynamic DNS hostname (e.g., yourdomain.no-ip.org).

Priority: This determines the priority of the mail server. If you only have one mail server, set it to 10 (a commonly used value). If you have multiple mail servers, use a lower number for the primary server and a higher number for backup servers.

Example MX record settings:

Host: @ (or mail, depending on your setup)

Points To: yourdomain.no-ip.org (replace this with your dynamic DNS hostname)

Priority: 10

Save the MX record changes.

Wait for DNS Propagation

After updating the MX record, DNS propagation might take up to 24-48 hours to take full effect across the internet.

However, it often happens more quickly (within an hour or two).

After the propagation time has passed, you can test whether your MX record is correctly configured by using the following methods:

Use an online DNS lookup tool to check your MX records:

You can use tools **like** MXToolbox - https://mxtoolbox.com/ or DNSstuff - https://www.dnsstuff.com/ to look up the MX records for your domain.

Test the connection using telnet

Open a terminal and run:

telnet yourdomain.no-ip.org 25

This will attempt to connect to your mail server via the SMTP port (25). If it connects, it indicates the MX record is pointing to the correct server.

Step 10: Open Firewall Ports

If your server has a firewall enabled, make sure to allow access to the necessary ports for IMAP, POP3, and their secure versions.

For UFW (Ubuntu/Debian), allow the ports:

sudo ufw allow 143/tcp

sudo ufw allow 993/tcp

sudo ufw allow 110/tcp

sudo ufw allow 995/tcp

For firewalld (CentOS/RHEL):

sudo firewall-cmd --permanent --add-port=143/tcp

sudo firewall-cmd --permanent --add-port=993/tcp

sudo firewall-cmd --permanent --add-port=110/tcp

sudo firewall-cmd --permanent --add-port=995/tcp

sudo firewall-cmd --reload

Spam Filtering with SpamAssassin

Spam is a common issue for any email server. To help reduce unwanted emails and ensure that your server is not marked as a spam source, we'll set up SpamAssassin, a powerful spam filtering tool.

Installing SpamAssassin: We'll cover how to install and

configure SpamAssassin on your server. Once installed, SpamAssassin will analyze incoming emails for potential spam and apply filters to reduce the volume of unsolicited emails.

Integration with Postfix: After installing SpamAssassin, we will show you how to integrate it with Postfix, so that Postfix will use SpamAssassin to filter incoming messages. You'll learn how to configure Postfix to check emails for spam and apply custom filtering rules based on your needs.

It is not recommended to set up SpamAssassin (or run an email server) on a dynamic IP. However, if your email server is intended for a small business with limited customer interaction—such as customers mainly contacting you through your website, or a small user base where email volume is low and deliverability isn't a critical concern—you may opt not to install SpamAssassin. This approach could work in cases where spam filtering isn't a top priority, but it's important to note that it might negatively impact your email reputation and deliverability.

The type of IP address (static or dynamic) can impact SpamAssassin in certain ways, particularly in how it handles email reputation, blacklisting, and how emails are received by your mail server.

Reputation and Blacklisting

Static IP:

A static IP remains the same over time. This consistency can be beneficial for your email reputation because services like SpamAssassin use various blacklists (DNS-based Blackhole List, or DNSBLs) to evaluate incoming emails. If your IP has a good reputation, email from your server is less likely to be flagged as spam.

On the flip side, if your static IP is associated with spam or blacklisted, it can cause your emails to be marked as spam by recipients.

Dynamic IP:

Dynamic IPs change periodically. This can make it challenging to build a good reputation with email services because each time your IP changes, SpamAssassin and other mail filters may treat your email with suspicion, as the IP may not have an established history.

Dynamic IPs are more commonly associated with residential

ISPs, which are often not trusted by email receivers. Emails sent from a dynamic IP address are more likely to be flagged as spam by spam filters because many spammer botnets use dynamic IP ranges to send out mass spam.

SPF (Sender Policy Framework) and Reverse DNS

Static IP:

A static IP makes it easier to set up a proper SPF record and reverse DNS (PTR) record, both of which are important for email deliverability.

An SPF record specifies which IPs are allowed to send email for your domain, helping to prevent spoofing. A reverse DNS record maps your IP to a domain name, providing additional verification that the sending server is legitimate.

SpamAssassin checks for these records, and a correct setup improves your email's reputation and deliverability.

Dynamic IP:

With a dynamic IP, maintaining a valid reverse DNS record and SPF record is more difficult because the IP address changes regularly.

Many dynamic IP addresses may not have valid reverse DNS or SPF records, leading SpamAssassin to flag emails as suspicious or spammy.

Some dynamic DNS services (like No-IP or DynDNS) can help mitigate this by updating the records automatically when your IP changes, but it's still a more complicated setup compared to a static IP.

Delivery to Major Providers:

Static IP: Providers like Gmail, Outlook, and Yahoo can build a history of your IP and trust it more over time if it's consistent.

Dynamic IP: Providers may be wary of emails coming from a frequently changing IP, especially if it is associated with residential ISPs, which are more prone to abuse and spam.

Blacklists and Whitelists:

Some blacklists target dynamic IP ranges specifically because they are more likely to be used by spammers and bots. This makes it harder for servers with dynamic IPs to get whitelisted.

If you're using a dynamic IP with SpamAssassin, you may find that emails are more likely to be flagged based on the IP's association with known spam sources, especially if the dynamic IP is shared or previously used for spamming activities.

For all the reasons mentioned, this section will focus solely on the installation and configuration of SpamAssassin for users with a static IP.

Step-by-Step Guide to Installing and Configuring SpamAssassin

Install SpamAssassin

SpamAssassin is available in the default repositories of most Linux distributions. You can install it using the package manager for your distribution.

For Ubuntu/Debian:

sudo apt update

sudo apt install spamassassin spamc

For CentOS/RHEL:

sudo yum install spamassassin

For Fedora:

sudo dnf install spamassassin

Enable SpamAssassin as a Service

By default, SpamAssassin does not run as a service. To enable it to start automatically, follow these steps:

For systemd-based systems:

sudo systemctl enable spamassassin

sudo systemctl start spamassassin

For older systems using init.d:

sudo service spamassassin start

```
sudo service spamassassin enable
```

Configure SpamAssassin

The default configuration of SpamAssassin works well for most users, but you may want to customize it for your specific needs. You can find the configuration file at /etc/spamassassin/local.cf.

Edit the configuration file:

```
sudo nano /etc/spamassassin/local.cf
```

Here are some useful settings you might want to adjust:

Required Score: Adjust the threshold score for marking a message as spam. The default is 5.0, meaning any email scoring above 5.0 will be marked as spam. You can adjust this value based on your preferences.

```
required_score 5.0
```

Enable Bayes Filtering: SpamAssassin uses a Bayesian filter to identify spam. Make sure it's enabled for better accuracy.

```
use_bayes 1
```

Auto Learn: Enable auto-learning to allow SpamAssassin to learn from your messages automatically.

bayes_auto_learn 1

Whitelist and Blacklist: You can add trusted senders to your whitelist and block known spam sources using blacklists. This can be done by adding entries like:

whitelist_from user@example.com

blacklist_from spam@example.com

After making your changes, save and exit the file.

Configure Your Mail Server to Use SpamAssassin

If you're running a mail server (like Postfix), you'll need to configure it to use SpamAssassin to filter incoming mail.

Configure Postfix to Use SpamAssassin: Postfix can call SpamAssassin through spamc (the SpamAssassin client). You need to add the necessary configuration to your mail server to invoke SpamAssassin on incoming mail.

First, make sure spamc is installed, which is included with the spamassassin package.

Now, edit your Postfix configuration file:

sudo nano /etc/postfix/main.cf

Add the following line:

content_filter = smtp-amavis:[127.0.0.1]:10024

Then configure the amavisd-new (which interfaces Postfix with SpamAssassin) service:

sudo apt install amavisd-new

Edit /etc/amavis/conf.d/15-content_filter_default:

$content_filter = 'smtp-amavis:[127.0.0.1]:10024';

Restart your services:

sudo systemctl restart postfix

sudo systemctl restart amavis

Test SpamAssassin

After configuration, you can test SpamAssassin by running it on an email message.

To manually test SpamAssassin on an email file, run the following:

spamassassin -t < /path/to/email/file

This command will output the results of SpamAssassin's evaluation of the email, including the spam score.

Check Logs

SpamAssassin logs its actions to /var/log/mail.log or /var/log/maillog (depending on your system). You can check these logs to troubleshoot any issues:

tail -f /var/log/mail.log

Additional Configuration Tips

Greylisting: You may also want to implement greylisting for additional spam prevention. This temporarily rejects email from unknown senders and forces them to resend, reducing spam.

RBL (Real-time Blackhole List) Configuration: You can configure SpamAssassin to check RBLs (such as zen.spamhaus.org or bl.spamcop.net) for known spammers.

To enable RBLs, add the following to local.cf:

use_rbls 1

Auto-learning: If you have a lot of legitimate emails that get caught as spam, you can manually train SpamAssassin to recognize these as non-spam, and vice versa.

Email Authentication

Email authentication protocols are essential to reduce spam and prevent spoofing. These protocols allow receiving mail servers to verify that emails are genuinely from the sender's domain and not forged.

SPF, DKIM, and DMARC: In this section, we will guide you

through the configuration of SPF (Sender Policy Framework), DKIM (DomainKeys Identified Mail), and DMARC (Domain-based Message Authentication, Reporting, and Conformance). These authentication methods prevent unauthorized users from sending emails from your domain and improve email deliverability by confirming that the messages are legitimate.

Testing Authentication: We'll provide tools and methods for testing the correct implementation of these authentication protocols, ensuring that your email server is properly configured to reduce spam and prevent domain spoofing.

Here's a detailed guide with examples for Email

Authentication Protocols (SPF, DKIM, and DMARC) that can help reduce spam, prevent spoofing, and improve email deliverability.

Email Authentication Protocols: SPF, DKIM, and DMARC

Email authentication protocols are essential for securing your domain and preventing unauthorized parties from sending emails that appear to come from your domain (spoofing). SPF, DKIM, and DMARC are the three key protocols that help verify email legitimacy. This guide will show you how to configure and test these protocols.

SPF (Sender Policy Framework)

SPF is a protocol that allows the domain owner to specify which mail servers are allowed to send emails on behalf of the domain. It helps receiving mail servers identify whether the sending mail server is authorized to send emails for that domain.

How to Set Up SPF:

Create or Update your DNS TXT record for SPF

Add the SPF record to your domain's DNS settings. This record specifies the IP addresses or mail servers that are allowed to send emails on behalf of your domain.

Example SPF Record

v=spf1 ip4:192.0.2.0/24 include:_spf.google.com ~all

v=spf1 indicates this is an SPF record.

ip4:192.0.2.0/24 allows the specified IP range to send emails on behalf of your domain.

include:_spf.google.com allows Google servers to send email for your domain (useful if you're using Gmail or Google Workspace).

~all marks any email from unauthorized servers as a "soft fail," meaning it will be flagged but still accepted.

Add this record to your domain's DNS settings:

Log in to your DNS provider's dashboard.

Add a TXT record with the above value.

Testing SPF

You can test your SPF record using online tools like:

MXToolbox SPF Lookup: https://mxtoolbox.com/spf.aspx

Kitterman SPF Tester:

http://www.kitterman.com/spf/validate.html

These tools will verify if your SPF record is properly configured.

DKIM (DomainKeys Identified Mail)

DKIM is an email authentication method that uses cryptographic signatures to verify that an email was sent by an authorized mail server and that its content has not been tampered with.

How to Set Up DKIM

Generate DKIM Keys

You will need to generate a private/public key pair for DKIM. The private key will be used by your mail server to sign outgoing messages, while the public key will be published in your DNS record.

If you're using Postfix and OpenDKIM, you can generate keys using the following command:

opendkim-genkey -s mail -d example.com

Add the Public Key to DNS

Add the generated DKIM public key to your domain's DNS settings as a TXT record. The key will look like this:

Example DKIM DNS Record:

mail._domainkey.example.com IN TXT ("v=DKIM1; k=rsa; p=MIGfMA0GCSq...AB")

mail._domainkey is the selector, which is used to look up the DKIM key.

v=DKIM1 indicates that this is a DKIM record.
k=rsa specifies the encryption method.
p=MIGfMA0...AB is the public key portion.

Configure your Mail Server

After generating the DKIM key, configure your mail server (like Postfix with OpenDKIM) to sign outgoing emails with the private key.

Example configuration for OpenDKIM on Postfix:

sudo nano /etc/opendkim.conf

Add the following lines to point to your private key and select your domain:

Domain   example.com

KeyFile   /etc/opendkim/keys/example.com.private

Selector   mail

Restart the Services

After configuring DKIM, restart your mail server and the DKIM service to apply changes:

```
sudo systemctl restart postfix

sudo systemctl restart opendkim
```

Testing DKIM

You can test DKIM using these tools:

MXToolbox DKIM Lookup:
https://mxtoolbox.com/dkim.aspx

DKIMValidator: https://www.dkimvalidator.com/

These tools will check if your DKIM signatures are being added and validated correctly.

DMARC (Domain-based Message Authentication, Reporting & Conformance)

DMARC allows domain owners to define how receiving mail servers should handle emails that fail SPF or DKIM checks. It also provides reporting mechanisms so that you can monitor authentication failures.

How to Set Up DMARC:

Create a DMARC Record

A DMARC record is added to your domain's DNS settings as a TXT record. This record will tell mail servers how to handle emails that fail SPF and/or DKIM checks.

Example DMARC Record:

v=DMARC1; p=reject; rua=mailto:dmarc-reports@example.com; ruf=mailto:dmarc-failures@example.com; pct=100

v=DMARC1 specifies the version of DMARC.

p=reject means that emails that fail DMARC checks should be rejected.

rua=mailto:dmarc-reports@example.com specifies where aggregate reports should be sent.

ruf=mailto:dmarc-failures@example.com specifies where forensic reports should be sent.

pct=100 means this policy applies to 100% of emails.

Add the DMARC Record to DNS

Add the DMARC record to your DNS provider's dashboard.

You'll need to add it as a TXT record under _dmarc:

_dmarc.example.com IN TXT "v=DMARC1; p=reject; rua=mailto:dmarc-reports@example.com; ruf=mailto:dmarc-failures@example.com; pct=100"

Testing DMARC

You can test your DMARC record using these tools:

MXToolbox DMARC Lookup:

https://mxtoolbox.com/dmarc.aspx

DMARC Analyzer: https://www.dmarcanalyzer.com/

These tools will help ensure your DMARC record is set up correctly and that emails are being handled according to your policies.

Testing Authentication

Once you've configured SPF, DKIM, and DMARC, it's important to test their functionality and make sure everything is set up properly. Here's how you can test your email authentication:

Send a Test Email

Send an email from your domain to an external email address (e.g., a Gmail account). In the email headers, check for the following:

SPF: Look for "spf=pass" in the header.

DKIM: Look for "dkim=pass" in the header.

DMARC: Look for "dmarc=pass" in the header.

Use Online Testing Tools

Mail-tester.com: https://www.mail-tester.com/ – This tool will test your SPF, DKIM, and DMARC setup and provide feedback.

MxToolbox Email Health: https://mxtoolbox.com/email-health/ – It checks all your email authentication settings.

Email Client Configuration

To ensure your users can send and receive emails from their desktop or mobile devices, we will configure email clients to securely connect to your server using IMAP and SMTP.

Setting Up Desktop and Mobile Email Clients: You'll learn how to configure popular email clients such as Thunderbird,

Outlook, and mobile devices (iOS/Android) to send and receive emails using your server. This includes setting up the correct IMAP/POP3 and SMTP settings to ensure secure communication with your server using encryption protocols.

Below are examples of how to configure desktop and mobile email clients (such as Thunderbird, Outlook, and mobile devices) for test@yourdomain.com, including IMAP/POP3 and SMTP settings, along with encryption protocols for secure communication.

Configuring Thunderbird (Desktop Email Client)

Account Settings for test@yourdomain.com:

Open **Thunderbird** and click on **"Email"** under the account setup wizard.

Enter your name, email address (**test@yourdomain.com**), and password for the email account.

Click **Continue**.

Incoming Server (IMAP) Settings:

Server Type: IMAP

Server Name: mail.yourdomain.com (This is your mail server's address)

Port: 993

Connection Security: SSL/TLS

Authentication Method: Normal Password

Username: test@yourdomain.com

Outgoing Server (SMTP) Settings:

SMTP Server: mail.yourdomain.com (Use your domain's mail server address)

Port: 587

Connection Security: STARTTLS (or SSL/TLS if you prefer)

Authentication Method: Normal Password

Username: test@yourdomain.com

Click **Done** to finish.

Configuring Outlook (Desktop Email Client)

Account Settings for test@yourdomain.com:

Open **Outlook** and go to **File > Add Account**.

Enter your name, email address (**test@yourdomain.com**), and password, then click **Next**.

IMAP/POP3 Incoming Settings:

Select **IMAP** or **POP3** for the incoming server (IMAP is recommended for syncing emails across devices).

Enter the following details:

Incoming Mail Server (IMAP): mail.yourdomain.com

Port: 993 (IMAP with SSL/TLS)

Username: test@yourdomain.com

Password: Your email password

SMTP Outgoing Settings:

Enter the following details for SMTP:

Outgoing Mail Server (SMTP): mail.yourdomain.com

Port: 587

Encryption Method: STARTTLS (or SSL/TLS for a higher security level)

Username: test@yourdomain.com

Password: Your email password

Click **Next**, let Outlook test the connection, and then click **Finish**.

Configuring iOS (iPhone or iPad) Email Client

Add Account for test@yourdomain.com:

Open the **Settings** app and go to **Mail > Accounts > Add Account**.

Select **Other** under the email provider options.

IMAP Incoming Server Settings:

Name: Your Name

Email: test@yourdomain.com

Password: Your email password

Description: Any description (e.g., "Personal Email")

For the incoming mail server:

Host Name: mail.yourdomain.com

User Name: test@yourdomain.com

Password: Your email password

Port: 993

SSL: On (for secure connection)

SMTP Outgoing Server Settings:

SMTP Server: mail.yourdomain.com

User Name: test@yourdomain.com

Password: Your email password

Port: 587

SSL: On

Authentication: Password

Click **Next** and **Save** to finish the setup.

Chapter 4: Configuring SSH for Secure Remote Access

What is SSH: Understanding the Importance of SSH for Secure Remote Access

Secure Shell (SSH) is a protocol used to securely access and manage remote servers over a network. It allows users to log in to a remote machine, execute commands, and transfer files through a secure, encrypted channel. Essentially, SSH provides you with a terminal to your Linux server from a remote location. By encrypting all traffic—such as passwords and commands—SSH ensures a high level of security, making it resistant to eavesdropping and man-in-the-middle attacks.

The importance of SSH in server management cannot be overstated, especially when administering a server over the internet. Unlike less secure methods, such as Telnet or FTP, SSH ensures that sensitive data remains private. Whether you're managing a web server, deploying applications, or troubleshooting, SSH is the primary method for secure, encrypted communication with a Linux server.

Installing and Configuring SSH

Installing OpenSSH Server:

The first step in configuring SSH for your Linux server is

installing the OpenSSH server, which is the software that enables SSH access. Most Linux distributions come with OpenSSH packages in their repositories, making the installation process quick and easy.

To install OpenSSH on a Debian-based system (such as Ubuntu), run the following command:

sudo apt update

sudo apt install openssh-server

For Red Hat-based systems (such as CentOS or Fedora), use:

sudo yum install openssh-server

After the installation, SSH should start automatically, but you can check its status and enable it to start on boot by running:

sudo systemctl status ssh

sudo systemctl enable ssh

To connect to your server remotely using SSH, you would run the following command from your local machine (replace your_server_ip with the server's IP address):

ssh username@your_server_ip

Configuring SSH Keys for Secure Login:

While password-based authentication is available, it's considered less secure than using SSH keys. SSH keys consist of a pair of cryptographic keys: a private key (kept on your local machine) and a public key (stored on the server). The private key never leaves your computer, and the server authenticates you by matching the public key with the private key during login attempts.

To configure SSH key-based authentication

Generate an SSH key pair on your local machine by running:

ssh-keygen

Follow the prompts to save the key (the default location is ~/.ssh/id_rsa).

Copy the public key to the server using the ssh-copy-id command:

ssh-copy-id username@your_server_ip

This will add your public key to the server's ~/.ssh/authorized_keys file.

Once this is done, you can log in to the server without entering a password. SSH will use your private key for authentication.

Disabling Root Login for Enhanced Security:

For security reasons, it's highly recommended to disable direct root login via SSH. By default, many systems allow direct login as the root user, but this can create a security risk if the root account is compromised.

To disable root login

Open the SSH configuration file (/etc/ssh/sshd_config) using a text editor like nano:

sudo nano /etc/ssh/sshd_config

Find the line containing PermitRootLogin and change its value to no:

PermitRootLogin no

Save the file and restart the SSH service to apply the changes:

sudo systemctl restart ssh

This configuration ensures that only non-root users can log in, which improves server security by reducing the potential for brute-force attacks on the root account.

SSH File Transfer Protocol (SFTP): Setting Up Secure File Transfers

SSH isn't just for logging in from remote and running commands; it also enables secure file transfers via the SSH File Transfer Protocol (SFTP). Unlike traditional FTP, which transmits data in plain text, SFTP encrypts both the commands and data, making it much more secure for transferring files over a network.

To use SFTP, you don't need to install any additional software on most Linux systems, as SFTP is usually included as part of the OpenSSH package.

To start an SFTP session, run:

sftp username@your_server_ip

Once connected, you can use commands like put (to upload files), get (to download files), and ls (to list files) to manage your server's files securely.

SFTP also supports recursive transfers, allowing you to transfer entire directories with the -r flag.

For example:

sftp> put -r /local_directory /remote_directory

This provides an easy and secure method for transferring data to and from your server.

Using SSH Tunneling: Introduction to SSH Tunneling for Secure Communication

SSH tunneling (also known as SSH port forwarding) is a powerful feature that allows you to create a secure, encrypted tunnel between your local machine and a remote server. This can be useful for accessing services or ports on the remote server that are otherwise blocked or restricted.

There are two main types of SSH tunneling:

Local Port Forwarding: This allows you to forward a local port on your machine to a remote port. For example, you can securely access a web application running on your server's private network through an encrypted tunnel.

ssh -L 8080:localhost:80 username@your_server_ip

This command forwards your local machine's port 8080 to the server's port 80, allowing you to access the server's web service via http://localhost:8080.

Remote Port Forwarding: This allows you to forward a remote port to a local machine or service. It's useful if you need to expose a service running on your local machine to the remote server.

ssh -R 8080:localhost:80 username@your_server_ip

This command forwards the server's port 8080 to your local machine's port 80, effectively allowing the remote server to access a service running locally.

SSH tunneling is a useful tool for securely bypassing network restrictions, creating secure access to internal services, or encrypting data for remote communication.

Chapter 5: FTP Server Setup

Why Use FTP: Understanding the Role of FTP in Web Hosting

File Transfer Protocol (FTP) is one of the oldest and most widely used methods for transferring files between a local computer and a remote server. In the context of web hosting, FTP is essential for uploading website files, managing directories, and downloading backups or logs. Whether you're maintaining a personal blog, running a complex eCommerce site, or handling a large project, FTP provides an easy-to-use method for managing your website's files remotely.

FTP allows webmasters and developers to work with their web server's file system without needing to access the server's command line interface directly. It is especially useful for bulk file transfers and managing large numbers of files, and it can be integrated with various automation tools and workflows. However, traditional FTP transmits data in plaintext, which can present security risks. To mitigate these risks, it is highly recommended to use a secure variant of FTP, such as FTPS or SFTP.

Installing vsftpd: Setting Up a Basic FTP Server

vsftpd (Very Secure FTP Daemon) is one of the most popular and secure FTP servers for Linux. It is known for its simplicity, high performance, and security features, making it an ideal choice for web hosting environments.

To install vsftpd on a Debian-based system (such as Ubuntu), run the following commands:

sudo apt update

sudo apt install vsftpd

For Red Hat-based systems (such as CentOS), use:

sudo yum install vsftpd

Once installed, vsftpd will start automatically. You can verify its status and ensure it starts on boot by running:

sudo systemctl status vsftpd

sudo systemctl enable vsftpd

Next, configure vsftpd by editing its main configuration file (/etc/vsftpd.conf):

sudo nano /etc/vsftpd.conf

A few basic settings to consider:

anonymous_enable=NO: Disable anonymous login (important for security).

local_enable=YES: Allow local users to log in.

write_enable=YES: Allow file uploads and modifications.

After modifying the configuration, restart the vsftpd service to apply changes:

sudo systemctl restart vsftpd

At this point, the FTP server should be ready to use for basic file transfers.

Securing FTP (FTPS): Configuring Secure FTP with SSL/TLS

While basic FTP is functional, it is insecure because data, including passwords, is transmitted in plaintext. To enhance security, you should configure FTPS (FTP Secure), which encrypts both the control and data connections using SSL/TLS. You can also use the same certificate you generated for your HTTPS setup.

To enable FTPS in vsftpd:

Generate an SSL certificate for your server:

```
sudo openssl req -new -x509 -days 365 -nodes -out
/etc/ssl/certs/vsftpd.pem -keyout /etc/ssl/private/vsftpd.key
```

Edit the vsftpd configuration file to enable SSL/TLS:

sudo nano /etc/vsftpd.conf

Modify the following settings:

```
# Enable SSL encryption.
ssl_enable=YES

# Disable SSL for anonymous users.
allow_anon_ssl=NO

# Require SSL for data connections.
force_local_data_ssl=YES

# Require SSL for login sessions.
force_local_logins_ssl=YES

# Specify the certificate file – you may use the same
# certificate you generated for your HTTPS here.
ssl_cert_file=/etc/ssl/certs/vsftpd.pem

# Specify the private key file – you may use the same key file
you generated for your HTTPS here.
ssl_key_file=/etc/ssl/private/vsftpd.key
```

Restart vsftpd to apply changes:

```
sudo systemctl restart vsftpd
```

Now, FTP traffic will be securely encrypted using SSL/TLS, protecting your data during transfer and preventing eavesdropping or tampering.

Managing FTP Access: Creating Users, Setting Permissions, and Troubleshooting

After setting up vsftpd, it's important to manage user access and permissions properly to ensure that users only have access to the files they need.

Creating FTP Users

To create a new FTP user, use the following command:

```
sudo adduser ftpuser
```

This creates a new user with a home directory. You can specify the user's permissions by editing the file system permissions or by modifying the vsftpd configuration to limit their access to certain directories.

Setting Permissions:

File and directory permissions are critical for controlling

access to files. You can use the chmod command to modify the permissions for files and directories:

```
sudo chmod 755 /path/to/directorysudo chmod 644 /path/to/file
```

These permissions ensure that only authorized users can modify files while others can read or execute them.

Troubleshooting FTP Access:

If you encounter issues with FTP access, the first step is to check the server's log files:

```
sudo tail -f /var/log/vsftpd.log
```

Additionally, ensure that the FTP server is running and accepting connections. If firewall issues are suspected, ensure the FTP port (usually port 21) is open on your server.

Connecting to FTP: Using FTP Clients (FileZilla, WinSCP) for File Management

Once your FTP server is configured and running, you can connect to it using an FTP client for easier file management. Two popular FTP clients are **FileZilla** (cross-platform) and **WinSCP** (for Windows).

Using FileZilla:

Open FileZilla and enter your server's IP address, the FTP username, and password in the appropriate fields.

Click **Quickconnect** to establish a connection to the server.

Use the graphical interface to upload, download, and manage files and directories on your server.

Using WinSCP:

Open WinSCP and choose **FTP** as the file protocol.

Enter the server IP address, FTP username, and password, then click **Login**.

Use the interface to drag and drop files between your local machine and the server.

Both of these FTP clients provide a user-friendly graphical interface to make file management on your server easier, offering drag-and-drop file transfers, directory synchronization, and much more.

Chapter 6: Setting Up a Print Server for Invoice Printing

Why Use a Print Server: Managing Printer Access Across Your Network

A print server is an essential tool for managing and sharing printers across multiple devices in a networked environment. Instead of connecting each computer directly to a printer, a print server allows multiple users and computers to access a single printer, improving efficiency and reducing the need for multiple devices. Print servers streamline the printing process by centralizing printer management, simplifying configuration, and providing better control over print jobs.

In a business or organizational setting, a print server can save time, reduce costs, and ensure that printers are shared efficiently. When dealing with invoices, which need to be printed on-demand and often in high volumes, having a dedicated print server makes the printing process seamless and automated. This chapter will guide you through setting up a Linux-based print server using CUPS (Common UNIX Printing System), adding network printers, and automating invoice printing.

Installing CUPS (Common UNIX Printing System): Setting Up a Print Server on Linux

CUPS is the default printing system for most Linux distributions, offering a simple yet powerful way to manage printers and print jobs. It supports a wide variety of printers, including both local and network printers, and integrates with other systems using various printing protocols like IPP, LPD, and SMB.

Installing CUPS:

To install CUPS on a Linux-based server, run the following commands:

Debian/Ubuntu-based systems:

sudo apt update

sudo apt install cups

Red Hat/CentOS-based systems:

sudo yum install cups

After installing CUPS, you need to start and enable the service so it runs automatically at boot:

sudo systemctl start cups

```
sudo systemctl enable cups
```

Next, check the status of the CUPS service to ensure it's running:

```
sudo systemctl status cups
```

CUPS also provides a web interface to manage printers, print jobs, and configurations. The CUPS web interface is typically accessible via http://localhost:631. You may need to configure firewall settings to allow access to this port from other computers on your network.

Configuring Network Printers: Adding Printers to the Server

Once CUPS is installed and running, the next step is to add your network printer(s) to the print server. The CUPS web interface provides a simple way to add printers.

Access the CUPS Web Interface: Open a browser and navigate to http://localhost:631. This will open the CUPS web interface.

Adding a Printer:

Click on **Administration** and then **Add Printer**.

You'll be prompted to authenticate as the root user (or an admin user) to proceed.

CUPS will scan for available printers on the network. If your printer is on the same network, it should appear in the list.

Select the printer and click **Continue**. If your printer does not appear, you can manually configure it by selecting the appropriate device URI (such as ipp://printer_ip_address or socket://printer_ip_address).

Configuring Printer Settings: After selecting the printer, you'll be asked to configure the printer settings, such as the printer's name, description, location, and printing options (e.g., color, duplex printing). Make sure to select the correct printer model or driver from the list of available drivers.

Setting Printer Permissions: You can also configure who is allowed to print to the printer by selecting Allow printing from all users or specifying user-specific permissions. This is essential if your print server will be used by multiple departments or individuals.

Testing the Printer: Once the printer is added, print a test page to ensure it's correctly configured. You can do this from the CUPS web interface or through the **lp** command:

```
lp -d printer_name testfile.txt
```

Sharing Printers: Setting Up Printers for Remote Access Across the Network

CUPS allows you to share printers across a network, making them available to other computers or devices. To share your printer with other users on the network:

Enable Printer Sharing

In the CUPS web interface, go to **Administration** > **Server Settings**.

Check the box next to **Share printers connected to this system** to enable printer sharing.

Click **Change Settings** to save the changes.

Configure Firewall Rules: If you're using a firewall, ensure that it allows access to the CUPS service (port 631) from

other computers. For example, to allow access on a UFW-managed server, run:

sudo ufw allow 631/tcp

sudo ufw reload

Accessing the Printer Remotely: On other computers on the same network, you can add the shared printer by going to the Printers section in the system settings. The printer should appear as available. If not, you can manually add the printer using the CUPS URL (http://your_server_ip:631).

Printing Invoices: Creating Scripts to Automatically Print Invoices

With your print server set up, you can automate the printing of invoices, which is particularly useful for businesses that need to print invoices on demand or as part of a workflow. Here's how you can automate invoice printing on a Linux server using custom scripts.

Create an Invoice Template: Design your invoice template using a standard format like PDF or PostScript. Many businesses use PDF for invoices because of its portability and professional appearance.

Write a Script to Print Invoices Automatically:

To print an invoice automatically, you can write a simple shell script that sends the invoice to the printer.

Here's an example script that prints a PDF invoice:

```bash
#!/bin/bash
# Print invoice automatically
INVOICE_PATH="/path/to/invoice.pdf"
PRINTER_NAME="Your_Printer_Name"

lp -d $PRINTER_NAME $INVOICE_PATH
```

This script uses the lp command to send the specified invoice file ($INVOICE_PATH) to the designated printer ($PRINTER_NAME). You can trigger this script from a cron job or an event-driven task to automate the printing process.

Setting Up a Cron Job: If you want invoices to be printed at specific times (e.g., hourly, daily, etc.), you can set up a cron job to run the script periodically. To do this, open the cron configuration:

```
crontab -e
```

Add a new line for your script, specifying the frequency and the script to execute. For example, to print invoices every day at 8 AM:

```
0 8 * * * /path/to/print_invoice.sh
```

Automating Invoice Printing from Web Applications: If you have a web application that generates invoices, you can modify the application to automatically trigger the printing script when an invoice is generated. This could be done using webhooks or by integrating with the backend server that calls the printing script.

Chapter 7: Payment Gateway Integration

What is a Payment Gateway: Understanding the Role in E-commerce

A payment gateway is a service that authorizes and processes online payments for e-commerce stores and websites. It acts as an intermediary between your website and the payment processor or bank, ensuring that sensitive financial information, such as credit card details, is transmitted securely between the customer and the payment processor.

In simpler terms, it's the digital counterpart of a point-of-sale terminal, enabling merchants to accept payments for goods and services online. Payment gateways handle the entire transaction flow, including authorization, fraud prevention, and security.

In e-commerce, integrating a reliable payment gateway is crucial for providing customers with a seamless and secure way to pay for products or services. Whether you're running an online store, subscription service, or any business that requires payments, integrating a payment gateway ensures that you can handle monetary transactions securely and efficiently.

Choosing a Payment Gateway: Overview of Popular Gateways

When selecting a payment gateway for your website, several factors need to be considered, such as transaction fees, supported countries, ease of integration, security, and the types of payment methods accepted. Here's an overview of some popular payment gateways:

Stripe:

Pros: Offers a wide range of APIs for integration, supports international payments, and allows businesses to accept various payment methods like credit/debit cards, Apple Pay, and Google Pay.

Cons: Transaction fees apply, and the API may require a learning curve for advanced features.

Best for: Businesses looking for flexible and customizable payment solutions.

PayPal:

Pros: Trusted by millions of users worldwide, easy to set up, and widely accepted. Offers both basic and advanced APIs for handling transactions.

Cons: Higher transaction fees for international payments, and limited customization options.

Best for: Small businesses or those with a large existing customer base on PayPal.

Square:

Pros: Easy integration, no monthly fees, and competitive transaction fees. Square also provides point-of-sale (POS) hardware, making it ideal for businesses with both physical and online stores.

Cons: Limited international support, and fewer customization options compared to Stripe.

Best for: Small businesses that need both online and offline payment solutions.

Setting Up Payment Gateway API

In this section, we'll dive into the details of integrating two popular payment gateways, **Stripe** and **PayPal**, into your website. We'll go over the step-by-step process for both.

Stripe API Integration: A Step-by-Step Example

Create a Stripe Account:

Go to the Stripe - https://stripe.com/ website and create a developer account.

Once registered, you'll be able to access your API keys (Publishable Key and Secret Key) from the **Dashboard**.

Install Stripe's PHP Library: To interact with the Stripe API, you'll need the official Stripe PHP library. Install it using Composer:

composer require stripe/stripe-php

Create the Payment Form: Your payment page will need a form that allows the user to enter their payment details (credit card information).

Here's an example of the form in HTML:

```
<form action="charge.php" method="POST">
  <script src="https://js.stripe.com/v3/"></script>
  <button type="submit">Pay with Stripe</button>
</form>
```

Handle the Payment on the Server

In your charge.php file, set up the server-side logic to handle the payment request:

```php
require 'vendor/autoload.php';


\Stripe\Stripe::setApiKey('your_secret_key');

// Create a payment intent
$paymentIntent = \Stripe\PaymentIntent::create([
    'amount' => 5000,  // Amount in cents (e.g., 5000 = $50.00)
    'currency' => 'usd',
]);

// Send client secret to the front end
echo json_encode(['clientSecret' => $paymentIntent->client_secret]);
```

Complete the Payment Process: On the front-end, use the Stripe JavaScript library to complete the payment process. Include the client secret from the PHP server, which is necessary to complete the transaction.

PayPal API Integration: A Step-by-Step Guide

Create a PayPal Developer Account:

Go to the PayPal Developer Portal and sign up for an account.

Create an application in the **My Apps & Credentials** section to get your **Client ID** and **Secret**.

Install PayPal's PHP SDK: To integrate PayPal, install the PayPal PHP SDK using Composer:

```
composer require paypal/rest-api-sdk-php
```

Set Up the PayPal Payment Flow: Create a payment button or form that initiates the PayPal payment process.

On the server-side, you'll need to create a payment object:

```php
require 'vendor/autoload.php';


$apiContext = new \PayPal\Rest\ApiContext(
   new \PayPal\Auth\OAuthTokenCredential(
      'your_client_id',    // Client ID
      'your_client_secret' // Client Secret
   )
);

// Create payment object
$payment = new \PayPal\Api\Payment();
```

// Configure payment details (e.g., amount, currency)

Redirect to PayPal: After creating the payment object, redirect the user to PayPal's approval page where they will confirm the transaction. Once the user confirms, PayPal will redirect them back to your site with the payment details.

Handle PayPal Payment Execution: After the user has approved the payment, execute the payment:

```php
$paymentExecution = new \PayPal\Api\PaymentExecution();
$paymentExecution->setPayerId($payerId);   // Get from the PayPal response

try {
    $payment->execute($paymentExecution, $apiContext);
} catch (Exception $e) {
    // Handle error
}
```

Handling Transactions with PHP

Now that the payment gateway is integrated, the next step is to handle transactions effectively. This includes securely processing payment information and storing transaction data.

Writing PHP Scripts to Handle Payments and Store Transaction Data

Store Transaction Data: When a payment is successful, store relevant details like the transaction ID, amount, customer information, and payment status in your database for record-keeping and future reference:

```
$sql = "INSERT INTO transactions (transaction_id, amount, status, customer_id) VALUES (?, ?, ?, ?)";

$stmt = $conn->prepare($sql);

$stmt->bind_param("ssss", $transactionId, $amount, $status, $customerId);

$stmt->execute();
```

Secure Payment Information with SSL: Ensure that the website where payment information is entered is secured with **SSL (Secure Sockets Layer)**. SSL encrypts sensitive data during transmission, protecting it from being intercepted. You can obtain an SSL certificate for your website through services like **Let's Encrypt** or commercial providers.

Handling Errors and Successes: For every transaction, handle both successes and failures.

For failed transactions, display a meaningful error message to the user:

```
if ($paymentSuccess) {

    echo "Payment Successful!";

} else {

    echo "Payment failed. Please try again.";

}
```

Testing Payment Integration: Using Sandbox Environments to Test Transactions

Both Stripe and PayPal provide sandbox environments that allow you to test payment transactions without using real money. Here's how you can test your integration:

Stripe:

In the Stripe dashboard, switch to **View test data**.

Use test card numbers (provided by Stripe) to simulate various transactions (e.g., successful payments, declines).

PayPal:

In the PayPal Developer Portal, create **sandbox accounts** for both the buyer and the seller.

Test transactions by logging in as the buyer and making payments to the seller sandbox account.

Chapter 8: Introduction to HTML and PHP for Website Development

Basic HTML Structure: Understanding the Basic Structure of an HTML Page

HTML (HyperText Markup Language) forms the foundation of every webpage. It is used to create the structure and content of a website. Understanding the basic HTML structure is essential for web development, as it allows you to organize and display information on the web.

Here is a breakdown of the core components of an HTML page:

Document Type Declaration: This declaration informs the browser which version of HTML is being used.

<!DOCTYPE html>

HTML Tags: The <html> tag encompasses the entire webpage content, marking the start and end of the document.

```
<html>
</html>
```

Head Section: The <head> tag contains meta-information about the document, like the title, character set, linked stylesheets, and external scripts.

```
<head>
   <meta charset="UTF-8">
   <title>My Website</title>
</head>
```

Body Section: The <body> tag contains the visible content of the webpage, such as text, images, and links.

```
<body>
   <h1>Welcome to My Website</h1>
   <p>This is my first webpage.</p>
</body>
```

Basic Structure Example:

```
<!DOCTYPE html>
<html>
   <head>
```

```
    <meta charset="UTF-8">
    <title>My Website</title>
  </head>
  <body>
    <h1>Welcome to My Website</h1>
    <p>This is a simple HTML page to get started.</p>
  </body>
</html>
```

This basic structure is the foundation of any HTML page. It helps browsers interpret and display content correctly.

Creating Your First HTML Page: A Beginner's Tutorial on HTML for Website Content

Creating a simple HTML page is a great way to start learning web development. Here is a step-by-step guide to building your first HTML page:

Create a new file: Open a text editor (such as Notepad, Sublime Text, or VS Code) and create a new file. Save it with a .html extension, for example, index.html.

Start with the DOCTYPE declaration:

```
<!DOCTYPE html>
```

Add the <html> tag to start the HTML document:

```
<html>
</html>
```

Inside the <html> tags, create the <head> section:

```
<head>
    <meta charset="UTF-8">
    <title>My First Webpage</title>
</head>
```

Add the <body> section: Here, you'll include the visible content such as headings, paragraphs, and links.

```
<body>
    <h1>Welcome to My First Webpage</h1>
    <p>Hello, world! This is my very first HTML page.</p>
    <a href="https://www.example.com">Visit Example</a>
</body>
```

Complete Example:

```
<!DOCTYPE html>
<html>
```

```html
<head>
    <meta charset="UTF-8">
    <title>My First Webpage</title>
  </head>
  <body>
    <h1>Welcome to My First Webpage</h1>
    <p>Hello, world! This is my very first HTML page.</p>
    <a href="https://www.example.com">Visit Example</a>
  </body>
</html>
```

View your page: Open the .html file in a web browser to see the page rendered. You'll see your heading, paragraph, and link.

By following these steps, you've created your first static webpage with HTML. This page will only display what is written in the code and does not change unless you manually edit it.

Dynamic Web Pages with PHP

PHP (Hypertext Preprocessor) is a server-side scripting language designed for web development. It enables you to create dynamic content that can change based on user input, databases, or other interactions. PHP is widely used for building interactive and database-driven websites.

How PHP Works with HTML

PHP can be embedded within HTML, allowing you to combine static content (HTML) with dynamic content (PHP). PHP code is processed on the server and sends the result to the browser as plain HTML.

Here's a simple example:

```
<!DOCTYPE html>
<html>
  <head>
    <meta charset="UTF-8">
    <title>Dynamic Page with PHP</title>
  </head>
  <body>
    <h1>Welcome to My Website</h1>
    <p>Today's date is: <?php echo date("Y-m-d"); ?></p>
  </body>
</html>
```

In this example, PHP is used to insert the current date dynamically into the page. The <?php echo date("Y-m-d"); ?>

part of the code generates the current date and displays it within the HTML.

Creating Simple PHP Scripts for Dynamic Content

Contact Forms: You can use PHP to process form submissions and store or email the data.

Example of an HTML form:

```
<form action="process_form.php" method="POST">
  <label for="name">Name:</label>
  <input type="text" id="name" name="name" required>
  <label for="email">Email:</label>
  <input type="email" id="email" name="email" required>
  <button type="submit">Submit</button>
</form>
```

In process_form.php, the PHP script would handle the form submission:

```
<?php

$name = $_POST['name'];

$email = $_POST['email'];

echo "Thank you, $name! Your email address is $email.";

?>
```

Blog Posts: PHP can be used to dynamically display content stored in a database, such as blog posts.

Example:

```php
<?php
// Database connection
$conn = new mysqli("localhost", "root", "", "my_database");

$sql = "SELECT title, content FROM posts";
$result = $conn->query($sql);

while ($row = $result->fetch_assoc()) {
    echo "<h2>" . $row['title'] . "</h2>";
    echo "<p>" . $row['content'] . "</p>";
}
?>
```

This script fetches and displays blog posts from the database.

Using PHP with MySQL: Introduction to Database-Driven Websites

To build dynamic websites, you often need to store and retrieve data. MySQL is a widely-used relational database management system, and PHP can interact with MySQL to create database-driven websites.

Connecting PHP to MySQL

Here's how you connect PHP to a MySQL database using the PDO extension:

```php
<?php
$servername = "localhost";
$username = "root";
$password = "";
$dbname = "my_database";

try {
    // Create PDO connection
    $conn = new PDO("mysql:host=$servername;dbname=$dbname", $username, $password);

    // Set the PDO error mode to exception
    $conn->setAttribute(PDO::ATTR_ERRMODE, PDO::ERRMODE_EXCEPTION);

    echo "Connected successfully";
} catch (PDOException $e) {
    // Catch and display any errors
    echo "Connection failed: " . $e->getMessage();
}
?>
```

Performing SQL Queries in PHP

You can retrieve data from the database and display it on your website:

```php
$sql = "SELECT title, content FROM blog_posts";
$result = $conn->query($sql);

if ($result->num_rows > 0) {
    while($row = $result->fetch_assoc()) {
        echo "<h2>" . $row['title'] . "</h2>";
        echo "<p>" . $row['content'] . "</p>";
    }
} else {
    echo "0 results";
}
```

This code fetches all blog posts from the database and displays them on the webpage.

Handling Forms with PHP: Writing PHP Code to Process HTML Form Submissions

Handling forms is one of the most common tasks in web development. With PHP, you can receive form submissions, validate the input, and process the data accordingly.

Processing a Simple Form with PHP

HTML Form - This form allows users to submit their name and email:

```
<form action="process_form.php" method="POST">
    <label for="name">Name:</label>
    <input type="text" id="name" name="name" required>
    <label for="email">Email:</label>
    <input type="email" id="email" name="email" required>
    <button type="submit">Submit</button>
</form>
```

PHP Script to Process Form:

```php
<?php
if ($_SERVER["REQUEST_METHOD"] == "POST") {
    $name = $_POST['name'];
    $email = $_POST['email'];

    // Simple validation
    if (!empty($name) && filter_var($email, FILTER_VALIDATE_EMAIL))
{
```

```php
    echo "Thank you, $name! We have received your email address:
$email.";

  } else {

    echo "Please fill in all fields correctly.";

  }

}

?>
```

This script validates the form data and outputs a message based on whether the input is valid.

Chapter 9: MySQL Setup and PDO for Database Integration

Installing MySQL/MariaDB: Setting Up a MySQL Database Server

MySQL (or its open-source fork MariaDB) is one of the most widely-used relational database management systems (RDBMS) for web development. It stores and organizes data in tables, and is commonly used in combination with PHP to create dynamic, data-driven websites.

Installing MySQL on Linux (Ubuntu/Debian)

To install MySQL (or MariaDB) on a Linux server:

Update Your System:

sudo apt update

sudo apt upgrade

Install MySQL Server: For MySQL:

sudo apt install mysql-server

For Debian - MariaDB (which is a community-driven fork of MySQL):

sudo apt install mariadb-server

Secure MySQL Installation - Run the mysql_secure_installation script to improve the security of your MySQL installation:

sudo mysql_secure_installation

Verify Installation - To check if MySQL is installed correctly, run:

mysql --version

Start the MySQL Service:

sudo systemctl start mysql

Enable MySQL to Start on Boot:

sudo systemctl enable mysql

Access MySQL - After installation, log in to MySQL as the root user:

sudo mysql -u root -p

Creating Databases and Tables: A Quick Guide to MySQL Commands

Once MySQL is installed and running, you need to create databases and tables to store your application data.

Creating a New Database

To create a database:

CREATE DATABASE my_database;

Creating a New Table

To create a table in your database:

USE my_database;

```
CREATE TABLE users (
    id INT AUTO_INCREMENT PRIMARY KEY,
    username VARCHAR(50) NOT NULL,
    email VARCHAR(100) NOT NULL,
    password VARCHAR(255) NOT NULL,
    created_at TIMESTAMP DEFAULT CURRENT_TIMESTAMP
);
```

This SQL command creates a users table with columns for id,

username, email, password, and a timestamp for when the user was created.

Inserting Data into the Table

To insert a new user into the users table:

```
INSERT INTO users (username, email, password)
VALUES ('john_doe', 'john@example.com', 'password123');
```

Querying Data

To retrieve data from the users table:

```
SELECT * FROM users;
```

You can also filter results using the WHERE clause:

```
SELECT * FROM users WHERE username = 'john_doe';
```

Updating Data

To update a user's email:

```
UPDATE users SET email = 'new_email@example.com' WHERE username = 'john_doe';
```

Deleting Data

To delete a user:

DELETE FROM users WHERE username = 'john_doe';

Introduction to PDO (PHP Data Objects): Using PDO for Secure Database Interactions

PHP Data Objects (PDO) is a database access layer that provides a uniform interface for working with multiple database types. PDO allows you to write secure, database-independent code.

Advantages of Using PDO:

Security: PDO provides built-in methods to handle prepared statements, which prevent SQL injection attacks.

Flexibility: You can use PDO to interact with multiple databases (MySQL, PostgreSQL, SQLite, etc.) without

changing your code.

Efficiency: PDO can handle large datasets and allows for better performance when working with databases.

Connecting PHP to MySQL with PDO

Setting Up a PDO Connection

To connect to a MySQL database using PDO, you need to create a PDO instance in PHP and pass in the connection parameters (database name, username, and password).

Here's an example:

```php
<?php
$host = '127.0.0.1'; // Database server
$db = 'my_database'; // Database name
$user = 'root'; // Database username
$pass = ''; // Database password

try {
    // Set up the PDO connection
    $pdo = new PDO("mysql:host=$host;dbname=$db", $user, $pass);
    // Set the PDO error mode to exception
    $pdo->setAttribute(PDO::ATTR_ERRMODE,
PDO::ERRMODE_EXCEPTION);

    echo "Connected to the database!";
} catch (PDOException $e) {
```

```php
    echo "Connection failed: " . $e->getMessage();

}
?>
```

This script will connect to the database using the mysql driver, with the specified parameters.

Writing PDO Scripts for Data Retrieval, Insertion, and Updates

Retrieving Data:

```php
<?php
$stmt = $pdo->query("SELECT id, username, email FROM users");

while ($row = $stmt->fetch(PDO::FETCH_ASSOC)) {
    echo $row['id'] . " - " . $row['username'] . " - " . $row['email'] .
"<br>";

}
?>
```

Inserting Data with Prepared Statements:

Prepared statements help prevent SQL injection attacks by separating SQL code from user input.

```php
<?php

$stmt = $pdo->prepare("INSERT INTO users (username, email,
password) VALUES (:username, :email, :password)");


$stmt->bindParam(':username', $username);

$stmt->bindParam(':email', $email);

$stmt->bindParam(':password', $password);


$username = "alice";

$email = "alice@example.com";

$password = password_hash("password123", PASSWORD_DEFAULT);

$stmt->execute();

?>
```

Updating Data with Prepared Statements:

```php
<?php

$stmt = $pdo->prepare("UPDATE users SET email = :email WHERE
username = :username");


$stmt->bindParam(':email', $email);

$stmt->bindParam(':username', $username);


$username = 'alice';

$email = 'new_email@example.com';
```

```php
$stmt->execute();

?>
```

Handling SQL Injection and Preventing Security Issues

To prevent SQL injection, always use prepared statements and parameterized queries. Never concatenate user input directly into SQL queries.

For example, the following is vulnerable to SQL injection:

```php
$sql = "SELECT * FROM users WHERE username = '$username'"; // DO NOT DO THIS!
```

Instead, use prepared statements:

```php
$stmt = $pdo->prepare("SELECT * FROM users WHERE username = :username");

$stmt->bindParam(':username', $username);

$stmt->execute();
```

Prepared statements safely handle user input by treating it as a value, not executable code.

Database Management: Using phpMyAdmin or MySQL Workbench to Manage Your Databases

phpMyAdmin:

phpMyAdmin is a web-based tool to manage MySQL databases. It provides a user-friendly interface to create databases, tables, and run SQL queries.

Installing phpMyAdmin:

sudo apt install phpmyadmin

Once installed, you can access phpMyAdmin through your browser (e.g., http://localhost/phpmyadmin).

Basic Functions:

Create and manage databases and tables

Run SQL queries

Import/export data

Manage user permissions and privileges

MySQL Workbench:

MySQL Workbench is a powerful desktop application for MySQL database administration. It provides tools for database design, SQL development, server administration, and more.

Installing MySQL Workbench: Download and install it from **the official website**:

https://dev.mysql.com/downloads/workbench/

Key Features:

Visual database design and modeling

Query execution and result visualization

Server management and configuration

Chapter 10: PHP Security Best Practices

Security is a critical concern when developing PHP applications, especially when dealing with user data, authentication, and online transactions. In this chapter, we will cover essential PHP security practices that will help you protect your application from various types of attacks, ensure secure communication, and safely manage user sessions and passwords.

Validating and Sanitizing User Input: Preventing Malicious Attacks

User input is one of the most common vectors for security vulnerabilities in web applications. Improper handling of user input can lead to Cross-Site Scripting (XSS), SQL Injection, and other malicious attacks. Therefore, validating and sanitizing all user input is essential to prevent these vulnerabilities.

Validating Input

Validation ensures that user input meets certain criteria before it is processed. You can validate input by checking for correct data formats, required fields, or even specific patterns (e.g., email addresses, dates).

Example: Validating an Email Address

```
$email = $_POST['email'];
if (filter_var($email, FILTER_VALIDATE_EMAIL)) {
    echo "Valid email address.";
} else {
    echo "Invalid email address.";
}
```

Sanitizing Input

Sanitization removes any unwanted characters or harmful code from user input. This process is especially important when dealing with input that may be displayed on a web page (to prevent XSS) or passed into SQL queries (to prevent SQL Injection).

Sanitizing a String for Display (Prevent XSS):

```
$name = $_POST['name'];

$name = htmlspecialchars($name, ENT_QUOTES, 'UTF-8');
// Converts special characters to HTML entities
```

Sanitizing Input for SQL Queries:

When using raw SQL queries, never directly insert user input into the query. Instead, use prepared statements to bind parameters securely.

```
$stmt = $pdo->prepare("SELECT * FROM users WHERE username = :username");

$stmt->bindParam(':username', $username);

$stmt->execute();
```

By using prepared statements with bound parameters, SQL injection is prevented.

Session Management: Securely Managing User Sessions with PHP

Sessions are a fundamental part of PHP applications that require user login functionality. However, improper session management can lead to session hijacking or session fixation attacks.

To securely manage sessions, follow these best practices:

Use Secure Cookies for Sessions

Ensure that session cookies are set to be secure and HTTPOnly. This prevents session cookies from being accessed by client-side JavaScript or transmitted over non-secure connections.

```php
// Start the session securely
session_start();

// Set session cookie parameters
session_set_cookie_params([
    'lifetime' => 0,
    'path' => '/',
    'secure' => true,  // Only send cookie over HTTPS
    'httponly' => true,  // Prevent access via JavaScript
]);

// Regenerate session ID to prevent session fixation
session_regenerate_id(true);
```

Avoid Storing Sensitive Information in Sessions

Do not store sensitive information such as passwords or credit card details directly in session variables. Instead, store only non-sensitive data and refer to a secure database for sensitive information.

Session Timeout

Implement session timeout to automatically log out users after a period of inactivity:

```php
// Set session timeout limit
$timeout_duration = 1800; // 30 minutes
if (isset($_SESSION['LAST_ACTIVITY']) && (time() -
$_SESSION['LAST_ACTIVITY'] > $timeout_duration)) {

    session_unset();    // Unset $_SESSION variable
    session_destroy();   // Destroy session
    echo "Session expired. Please log in again.";
}
$_SESSION['LAST_ACTIVITY'] = time(); // Update last activity time
```

Password Hashing: Storing Passwords Securely Using PHP's password_hash() Function

One of the most critical aspects of PHP security is how you store user passwords. Storing passwords in plaintext is a significant security risk. Instead, use PHP's password_hash() function to securely store hashed passwords, and password_verify() to check the password during login attempts.

Hashing Passwords

The password_hash() function uses a strong hashing algorithm (bcrypt by default) to securely hash passwords.

```
$password = $_POST['password'];

$hashed_password = password_hash($password,
PASSWORD_DEFAULT);
```

PASSWORD_DEFAULT ensures that the password is hashed using the current default algorithm (bcrypt).

The generated hash will include a salt, which adds an additional layer of security.

Verifying Passwords

When a user logs in, use the password_verify() function to check if the entered password matches the stored hash.

```
$entered_password = $_POST['password'];

$stored_hash = // Fetch hash from the database
```

```php
if (password_verify($entered_password, $stored_hash)) {
    echo "Login successful!";
} else {
    echo "Invalid credentials.";
}
```

Updating Passwords

When users change their password, hash the new password using password_hash() and update the stored hash in the database.

SSL/TLS for Secure Connections: Enforcing HTTPS for Secure Communication

One of the most important security practices for modern web applications is using SSL/TLS encryption to ensure secure communication between the user's browser and your server. This protects sensitive information such as passwords, credit card details, and personal data from being intercepted by attackers.

Enforcing HTTPS with PHP

To enforce HTTPS, you can use PHP to redirect users from

HTTP to HTTPS, ensuring that all traffic between the client and server is encrypted.

```php
if ($_SERVER['HTTPS'] !== 'on') {

    $url = "https://" . $_SERVER['HTTP_HOST'] . $_SERVER['REQUEST_URI'];

    header("Location: $url");

    exit();
}
```

Install and Configure an SSL Certificate

To enable HTTPS, you'll need to obtain and install an SSL certificate. You can get a free SSL certificate from Let's Encrypt, or purchase one from a trusted certificate authority (CA).

Install the certificate on your server.

Configure your web server (e.g., Apache, Nginx) to use SSL by modifying the server's configuration files.

Error Handling and Logging: Implementing Error Logging and Debugging Strategies

Error handling and logging are essential for debugging your PHP applications and detecting potential security issues. Proper error management can also prevent exposing sensitive information to end users.

Error Reporting

During development, you may want to display all errors for debugging purposes. However, in a production environment, you should suppress detailed error messages and instead log them to a secure file.

```
// Display errors during development
ini_set('display_errors', 1);
error_reporting(E_ALL);
```

```
// Log errors in production environment
ini_set('display_errors', 0);
ini_set('log_errors', 1);
ini_set('error_log', '/path/to/error_log');
```

Logging Errors

Log errors to a file or a remote logging service (such as Sentry, Loggly, or Papertrail) to track issues over time and analyze potential security breaches.

```php
// Log critical errors to a file
if ($error) {
    error_log("Critical Error: $error", 3, '/path/to/error_log');
}
```

Handling Exceptions

Use try-catch blocks to handle exceptions and provide meaningful error messages without revealing sensitive information:

```php
try {
    // Code that might throw an exception
    $pdo = new PDO($dsn, $username, $password);
} catch (PDOException $e) {
    // Log the exception
    error_log("Database connection failed: " . $e->getMessage());
    // Display a generic error message to the user
    echo "An error occurred. Please try again later.";
}
```

Chapter 11: Server Monitoring and Maintenance

Server monitoring and maintenance are critical tasks for keeping your server running efficiently and securely. Whether it's for a web server, database server, or any other type of server, proactive monitoring, automated backups, regular updates, and log management are essential for ensuring uptime and performance while safeguarding against data loss or security vulnerabilities. This chapter will explore the tools and strategies you can use to monitor and maintain your server effectively.

Setting Up Server Monitoring Tools: Tools like Nagios, Monit, or Netdata for Real-Time Server Monitoring

Monitoring your server in real-time helps you stay on top of its health and performance. Monitoring tools can track resource usage, detect issues, and notify administrators about potential problems. Here, we'll explore a few powerful server monitoring tools:

Nagios: A Comprehensive Monitoring Solution

Nagios is an open-source monitoring tool that allows you to

monitor various systems, including servers, applications, and network devices. It provides real-time monitoring and alerting, with extensive plugins for different types of services.

Steps to install Nagios on a Linux server:

Install Nagios and Dependencies - On a Debian/Ubuntu server, you can install Nagios by running:

sudo apt update

sudo apt install nagios4 nagios-plugins

Configure Nagios: After installation, you can configure Nagios by editing configuration files to define what services you want to monitor (e.g., CPU, RAM, disk usage, or specific applications like Apache or MySQL).

Accessing Nagios Web Interface: You can access Nagios' web interface at http://your-server-ip/nagios after completing the installation.

Monit: A Lightweight Monitoring Tool

Monit is a simple and lightweight monitoring tool that can automatically restart services or notify you when a service fails or is underperforming. It's especially useful for monitoring small servers or specific services like web servers and databases.

Steps to install and configure Monit:

Install Monit - On a Debian-based system, install Monit with the following command:

sudo apt install monit

Configuration: The main configuration file for Monit is located at /etc/monit/monitrc. You can edit this file to define services that you want to monitor, such as:

check process apache with pidfile /var/run/apache2.pid

start program = "/etc/init.d/apache2 start"

stop program = "/etc/init.d/apache2 stop"

Start Monit: Start the Monit service by running:

sudo systemctl start monit

Netdata: Real-Time Monitoring with a Web Interface

Netdata is an open-source, real-time monitoring tool that provides detailed performance metrics on your system, applications, and network. It comes with an interactive web interface, making it easy to visualize server health.

Steps to install Netdata:

Install Netdata: On a Debian-based system:

sudo apt install netdata

Access the Web Interface: After installation, you can access the Netdata dashboard at http://your-server-ip:19999.

Automating Backups: Using rsync, Cron, or Other Backup Solutions to Automate Backups

Regular backups are crucial for data protection and disaster recovery. Automating backups ensures that your server data is regularly backed up without requiring manual intervention.

Using rsync for Backup

rsync is a fast and reliable file synchronization tool that can be used for backups. It only transfers the differences between source and destination, making it efficient.

Steps to create an automated backup with rsync:

Create a Backup Script - Create a script (backup.sh) that uses rsync to copy files from a source directory to a backup destination:

```
#!/bin/bash
rsync -avz /var/www/html/ /backup/website/
```

Make the Script Executable:

```
chmod +x /path/to/backup.sh
```

Set Up Cron Jobs for Automation: You can schedule this script to run at regular intervals using cron. Edit the crontab:

```
crontab -e
```

Add the following line to run the backup script every day at midnight:

```
0 0 * * * /path/to/backup.sh
```

Using Other Backup Solutions

There are several third-party tools that can help automate backups, such as **Duplicity** (for encrypted backups) or **Bacula** (for enterprise-level backup solutions). These tools often provide additional features like backup scheduling, cloud storage support, and recovery tools.

Updating and Patching: Managing System Updates and Applying Patches

Regular system updates and patches are vital to maintaining the security and stability of your server. Keeping your system up to date protects against vulnerabilities and ensures that you benefit from the latest features and bug fixes.

Updating Linux Packages

On a Linux-based server, you can update your system packages using package managers like apt (for Debian/Ubuntu) or yum (for CentOS/RHEL). For example:

Debian/Ubuntu:

sudo apt update && sudo apt upgrade -y

CentOS/RHEL:

sudo yum update -y

Automating Updates

To automatically install security patches or updates, you can configure your server to use unattended upgrades. This feature is available on many Linux distributions and can be set up using the following:

Debian/Ubuntu:

sudo apt install unattended-upgrades

sudo dpkg-reconfigure unattended-upgrades

This will automatically download and install security updates without requiring manual intervention.

Log Management: Analyzing and Managing Logs for Security and Performance Monitoring

Logs provide valuable insights into your server's health and security status. Analyzing logs helps you identify issues before they become serious problems, as well as track down security breaches or abnormal behavior.

Log Files Location

On most Linux systems, log files are stored in the /var/log directory. Some of the key logs to monitor include:

/var/log/auth.log: Authentication-related logs (login attempts, sudo usage).

/var/log/syslog: General system logs.

/var/log/apache2/access.log and
/var/log/apache2/error.log: Web server logs.

/var/log/mysql/error.log: MySQL database logs.

Viewing Logs

You can view logs using commands like cat, less, or tail:

sudo tail -f /var/log/syslog # Real-time log monitoring

Using Log Management Tools

For more sophisticated log analysis, you can use tools like **Logrotate** (to manage log file size and rotation) and ELK Stack (Elasticsearch, Logstash, Kibana) for centralized logging and visualization.

Logrotate Configuration: Logrotate automatically rotates logs, archives them, and deletes old logs to prevent log files from consuming too much disk space.

To configure log rotation for a specific log file, edit /etc/logrotate.d:

```
/var/log/syslog {
    weekly
    rotate 4
    compress
    delaycompress
    missingok
    notifempty
    create 0640 root root
}
```

Chapter 12: Troubleshooting and Optimizing Your Server

Maintaining and optimizing a server is a continual process of monitoring, troubleshooting, and making adjustments to ensure high performance, security, and reliability. This chapter will cover common server issues and how to troubleshoot them, performance tuning for key services like Apache, NGINX, MySQL, and PHP, security auditing using essential tools, and best practices for keeping your website and server secure.

Common Server Issues: Troubleshooting Network, DNS, and Server Issues

Network Issues

Network-related problems are some of the most common issues you'll face with a server. These issues can range from slow connections to total network outages.

Common network issues:

Ping Failures: If you can't ping your server or get a timeout response, it could be due to a firewall blocking ICMP packets or network configuration issues.

DNS Resolution Problems: Your server may fail to resolve domain names, often due to issues with DNS settings or misconfigured /etc/resolv.conf on Linux systems.

Network Congestion: High traffic volumes or misconfigured networking settings may lead to network congestion.

Troubleshooting network issues:

Check Server Connectivity: Use tools like ping or traceroute to check network connectivity.

ping -c 4 google.com

traceroute google.com

Check Firewall Settings: Ensure your firewall is not blocking essential traffic.

sudo ufw status

sudo iptables -L

DNS Issues

DNS problems often arise from incorrect configurations or server issues.

Troubleshooting DNS issues:

Verify DNS Settings: Ensure your DNS resolver is correctly configured in /etc/resolv.conf for Linux systems. You can also check if DNS resolution is functioning using dig or nslookup.

dig google.com

nslookup google.com

Check DNS Server: Test the DNS server using dig with the @ operator to query a specific DNS server.

dig @8.8.8.8 google.com

Server Issues

Server-side issues can cause application downtime, poor performance, or even crashes.

Common server issues:

High CPU/Memory Usage: Excessive resource usage can slow down or crash the server.

Disk Space Issues: Running out of disk space can cause the server to malfunction.

Service Failures: Misconfigured or unresponsive services (like Apache, MySQL, or PHP-FPM) can lead to downtime.

Troubleshooting server issues:

Check Resource Usage: Use top, htop, or vmstat to identify processes that are consuming excessive resources.

top

htop

vmstat

Check Disk Space: Use the df and du commands to monitor disk usage.

df -h

du -sh /var/www/

Restart Failed Services: Restart services like Apache or MySQL if they're unresponsive.

sudo systemctl restart apache2

sudo systemctl restart mysql

Performance Tuning: Optimizing Apache/NGINX, MySQL, and PHP Configurations

Optimizing your server's performance is crucial for handling traffic efficiently and ensuring fast response times for users. Let's take a look at how you can optimize key services like Apache/NGINX, MySQL, and PHP.

Apache/NGINX Optimization

Both Apache and NGINX are popular web servers, and tuning their configurations is essential for high performance.

Apache optimization tips:

Enable KeepAlive: Keep connections open between the server and client to reduce latency.

KeepAlive On

MaxKeepAliveRequests 100

KeepAliveTimeout 5

Optimize MPM: Apache uses different Multi-Processing Modules (MPM) for handling requests. For example, use mpm_event or mpm_worker for better performance on high-traffic sites.

LoadModule mpm_event_module modules/mod_mpm_event.so

NGINX optimization tips:

Worker Processes and Connections: Adjust worker_processes and worker_connections for handling more traffic.

worker_processes 4;

worker_connections 1024;

Caching: Set up caching to reduce the load on the server and speed up response times.

proxy_cache_path /tmp/nginx_cache levels=1:2 keys_zone=cache_zone:10m max_size=10g;

MySQL Optimization

MySQL is at the heart of many web applications, and optimizing its performance can drastically improve query speeds and reduce load.

MySQL optimization tips:

Configure Buffer Sizes: Increase the innodb_buffer_pool_size to improve read/write speeds.

innodb_buffer_pool_size = 2G

Optimize Queries: Ensure that queries are optimized, use indexes, and avoid SELECT * queries.

Enable Query Cache: Use the query cache for faster retrieval of frequently executed queries.

query_cache_type = 1

query_cache_size = 64M

PHP Optimization

PHP is the engine behind many dynamic websites, and optimizing it helps ensure fast page loads.

PHP optimization tips:

Increase Memory Limits: For resource-heavy applications, increase memory_limit.

memory_limit = 256M

Enable OPcache: OPcache can significantly improve the performance of PHP scripts by caching the compiled bytecode in memory.

opcache.enable = 1

opcache.memory_consumption = 128

Configure Error Logging: Set up error logging to capture errors without displaying them to users.

log_errors = On

error_log = /var/log/php_errors.log

Security Auditing: Using Tools like Fail2ban, ClamAV, and Lynis to Secure the Server

A key part of server management is performing regular security audits to identify vulnerabilities and mitigate risks.

Fail2ban: Protecting Against Brute-Force Attacks

Fail2ban is an intrusion prevention software framework that protects servers from brute-force attacks by blocking IPs that repeatedly fail login attempts.

Steps to configure Fail2ban:

Install Fail2ban:

sudo apt install fail2ban

Configure Jail Settings: Edit /etc/fail2ban/jail.local to define which services to monitor (e.g., SSH, Apache, NGINX).

[sshd]

enabled = true

port = ssh

maxretry = 3

bantime = 600

Start Fail2ban:

```
sudo systemctl enable fail2ban

sudo systemctl start fail2ban
```

ClamAV: Virus Scanning for Linux Servers

ClamAV is an open-source antivirus software for scanning files and directories for viruses and malware.

Steps to install ClamAV:

Install ClamAV:

```
sudo apt install clamav clamav-daemon
```

Run a Virus Scan:

```
clamscan -r /var/www/html
```

Lynis: A Security Auditing Tool

Lynis is a security auditing tool that checks your server for potential vulnerabilities, configuration issues, and best practices.

Steps to run a Lynis security audit:

Install Lynis:

```
sudo apt install lynis
```

Run a Security Scan:

sudo lynis audit system

Keeping Your Website Secure: Best Practices for Maintaining a Secure Server and Website

Regular Updates

Keep your server and all software up to date. Regular updates ensure that you're protected against known vulnerabilities and threats.

Use package managers like apt (Debian/Ubuntu) or yum (CentOS/RHEL) to update software.

Automate security updates using tools like unattended-upgrades for Debian-based systems.

Strong Authentication

Always use strong, unique passwords for your server accounts, and enable two-factor authentication (2FA) for additional security. Secure SSH keys with strong passphrases and disable password authentication for SSH.

Secure File Permissions

Ensure that only the necessary users and groups have access to critical files and directories. Use tools like chmod and chown to restrict file access.

```
chmod 644 /var/www/html/index.php

chown www-data:www-data /var/www/html/index.php
```

Web Application Firewall (WAF)

Install and configure a WAF to filter and monitor HTTP traffic to and from your server. A popular option is ModSecurity, which can prevent SQL injection, cross-site scripting (XSS), and other attacks.

Appendices

A. Useful Linux Commands for Web Hosting

Linux is the backbone of many web hosting environments, and knowing the right commands can make managing a web server much easier. Below are some essential Linux commands for web hosting and server management.

File System and Permissions

ls: List directory contents.

ls -l

cd: Change directory.

cd /var/www/html

chmod: Change file permissions.

chmod 755 index.php

chown: Change file owner and group.

chown www-data:www-data index.php

find: Search for files in a directory hierarchy.

find /var/www -name "*.php"

Process Management

ps: List running processes.

ps aux

top: Monitor system resource usage in real-time.

top

kill: Terminate a process by its PID.

kill 12345

Networking

ping: Test network connectivity.

ping google.com

ifconfig: Display or configure network interfaces.

ifconfig

netstat: Show network connections, routing tables, interface statistics.

netstat -tuln

Service Management

systemctl: Manage system services (start, stop, restart).

sudo systemctl restart apache2

service: Manage services in older systems.

sudo service apache2 restart

Package Management

apt-get (Debian/Ubuntu) / **yum** (CentOS/RHEL): Install, remove, or update packages.

sudo apt-get install apache2

sudo yum install apache2

Disk Usage

df: Display disk space usage.

df -h

du: Estimate file space usage.

du -sh /var/www/

Backup and Restore

tar: Archive files and directories.

tar -czvf backup.tar.gz /var/www/

rsync: Sync files and directories between local and remote locations.

rsync -av /var/www/ user@server:/backup/

B. Glossary of Terms

Apache

A popular open-source web server software used to serve dynamic and static websites.

PHP

A server-side scripting language widely used for web development, allowing dynamic content generation.

MySQL

An open-source relational database management system (RDBMS) used to store data for websites.

SQL Injection

A type of security vulnerability that allows an attacker to interfere with the queries an application makes to its database.

SSL/TLS

Protocols used to secure communications over a computer network, typically used to implement HTTPS.

DNS (Domain Name System)

The system that translates domain names (like example.com) into IP addresses that computers can use to identify each other on the network.

FTP (File Transfer Protocol)

A protocol used to transfer files between computers over a network.

PHP Data Objects (PDO)

A database access library in PHP that provides a uniform and secure way to interact with databases.

OPcache

A caching engine built into PHP that improves performance by storing precompiled script bytecode in memory.

Cron

A time-based job scheduler in Unix-like operating systems used to schedule jobs like backups and system maintenance.

C. Troubleshooting Common Issues

As a web hosting administrator, you may encounter a variety of issues. Below are some common server problems and how to troubleshoot them.

Website Not Loading

Check Service Status: Ensure the web server (Apache or NGINX) is running.

sudo systemctl status apache2

Check Logs: Review web server logs for any errors.

tail -f /var/log/apache2/error.log

Check Disk Space: Ensure the server has enough disk space.

df -h

Database Connection Issues

Check MySQL Service: Ensure the MySQL service is running.

sudo systemctl status mysql

Verify Database Credentials: Double-check the username, password, and database host configured in your PHP code.

Check MySQL Logs: Review MySQL error logs for issues.

tail -f /var/log/mysql/error.log

Permission Denied Errors

File Permissions: Ensure files and directories have the correct permissions.

chmod 755 /var/www/html

chown www-data:www-data /var/www/html

SELinux Issues: If using SELinux, ensure that the context is correct.

restorecon -Rv /var/www/

Server High Load or Slow Performance

Check System Resources: Use top or htop to monitor CPU and memory usage.

top

htop

Optimize Database Queries: Review and optimize slow database queries.

SSL/TLS Certificate Issues

Verify Certificate: Check SSL/TLS certificate installation using tools like openssl.

openssl s_client -connect example.com:443

Check Expiry Date: Ensure the SSL certificate is not expired.

openssl x509 -enddate -noout -in /etc/ssl/certs/example.com.crt

D. Additional Resources (Web Development, MySQL, PHP, etc.)

Here are some useful online resources to deepen your knowledge and skills in web development, server management, and programming.

Web Development

MDN Web Docs: A comprehensive resource for learning HTML, CSS, and JavaScript.
https://developer.mozilla.org/

W3Schools: A great platform for tutorials on web technologies, including HTML, CSS, JavaScript, PHP, and more.
https://www.w3schools.com/

CSS-Tricks: Offers guides, tutorials, and examples on web design and front-end development.
https://css-tricks.com/

MySQL

MySQL Documentation: The official MySQL documentation for in-depth understanding of MySQL's features and functions.
https://dev.mysql.com/doc/

PHPMyAdmin: A free software tool for managing MySQL databases through a web interface.
https://www.phpmyadmin.net/

MySQL Performance Blog: Insights on optimizing MySQL performance from experts.
https://www.percona.com/blog/

PHP

PHP Manual: The official PHP manual for function references and tutorials.
https://www.php.net/manual/en/

PHP: The Right Way: A great resource for learning best practices in PHP development.
https://phptherightway.com/

Linux Administration

Linux Academy: Offers online courses for Linux and server administration.
https://linuxacademy.com/

DigitalOcean Tutorials: Tutorials for web hosting, server administration, and development.
https://www.digitalocean.com/community/tutorials

Server Fault: A Q&A site for system administrators and web hosting professionals.
https://serverfault.com/

www.ingramcontent.com/pod-product-compliance
Lightning Source LLC
LaVergne TN
LVHW022340060326
832902LV00022B/4151